Apocalyptic Anointing

Rony M. Reyes

Pickstone Religious Publications

Apocalyptic Anointing

Copyright © 2008 Rony M. Reyes

Printed in the United States of America on acid-free paper. All rights reserved. No part of this book may be reproduced, or stored in a retrieval system or transmitted in any form or by any means, electronic, mechanical, photocopying, recording, scanning or otherwise, except as permitted by the 1976 United States CopyrightAct, or with the prior written permission of Pickstone Religious Publications, P. O. Box 23961, Lexington, KY 40523.

Library of Congress Control Number 2008936905

ISBN   978-0-9797935-6-1

Cover photograph is by Courtesy of Los Alamos National Laboratory, Jack Aeby, photographer.

Contents

Preface   9

Introduction   13

Chapter 1. The Call   19

Chapter 2. Apocalyptic Pneumatology   31

Chapter 3. Various Expressions of the Apocalyptic Anointing   47

Chapter 4. Interpreting Apocalyptic Dreams and Visions   61

Chapter 5. Apocalyptic Symbolism and Warfare   77

Chapter 6. Third Level Spiritual Warfare   91

Chapter 7. Walking in the Apocalyptic Anointing   105

Select Bibliography   117

About the Author   119

Dedication

I dedicate this book to those who have sensed the calling of God to go beyond the norm. This book is for those who have been rejected and opposed for using their spiritual gifts in the local church. I pray that you will be encouraged and uplifted as you read.

I also dedicate this book to my wife, Hope, and children, Gabriel and Olivia—they have played a very important, supporting role during the writing process. Hours spent discussing, questioning, and challenging me to expound my thoughts and articulate my ideas. Thank you for your faith in this work and for your understanding!

Finally, I dedicate this book to my dear pastor, Gabriel Willis, who passed away several years ago. He was my first mentor in my Christian walk and my mentor in developing my spiritual gifts. One day, we will dine together with Christ Jesus the Lamb of God.

Acknowledgement

Since I became a Christian, countless numbers of people have spoken "inspired revelations" with regard to my ministry and calling. Many I have come to know, and others simply spoke the words that I needed to hear. To those who have spoken the inspired words of the Spirit into my life I say, "Thank you for obeying the Lord."

To those who have become my spiritual mentors, you have allowed God to use you and give you the words to speak into my life. You have challenged me in different aspects of my spiritual and intellectual growth and, because of your combined investment I continue to strive for a wholistic Christian living. To Dr. Amos Yong, for demonstrating outstanding Pentecostal scholarship. To Dr. David Andersen, for his love and support. You affirmed who I am and enabled me to see the Holy Spirit at work outside of Pentecostal/Charismatic traditions. To Cindy Bilski, for helping make sense of new revelations. Thank you for your intercessory and warfare prayers.

I would also like to acknowledge my wife, Hope, for helping to clean up the manuscripts of this book. I want to thank, Aprille Schutte, for helping edit and providing insight.

Preface

My purpose for writing this book is threefold. First, I want to encourage and affirm those who have unique gifts and are able to see in the realm of the Spirit. I would like to let them know that they are not alone; there are other gifted people who are able to see in the realm of the Spirit. Secondly, we need to be concrete with our experiences, to make sure that our experiences are backed up with the word of God. Third, I want to explore an understanding that, even though God moves in the spiritual world, he also desires us to be academic. We must allow God to refine our intellect and renew our mind.

Often, churches have not allowed individuals to use their spiritual gifts and rejected them. This book is also for those who might be interested in finding out more about the anointing of the Spirit, the gifts, and the spiritual fight that goes on day and night in the earth, under the earth, and in the heavenlies. My prayer is that this book might bring clarity regarding spiritual warfare to your spirit and your mind.

This book is about spiritual renewal, personally and corporally. Let us not forget the challenge that Patricia King brings in her book, *Spiritual Revolution: Experience the Supernatural in Your Life*. King says, "…religion of the 21st century and its parched, spiritless theology has very little to offer to modern man who seeks a spirituality that is high above the rationalism of our day…how can we, the Church of the living God, sit back and watch the enemy deceive with false signs, wonders, and miracles? How can we be complacent and powerless at such a critical time in history?"[1] Although we realize that there is a challenge when one writes about spiritual matters, it is important to remember that God wants to pour out his Spirit and give us his riches in glory. We cannot remain powerless.

Many years ago, as I began to study about the anointing, spiritual gifts, and spiritual warfare, I was overwhelmed by the many views on these subjects. Although there might be some danger or error in these views, one must be careful not to dismiss their authenticity altogether. Repeatedly, I have sat down with individuals who have been either misinformed or hurt by those who profess to have the ministry of spiritual warfare, a prophetic ministry, or the ministry of deliverance. This project does not solve all the unresolved issues on this subject; however, it should bring clarity to them.

Also this book was inspired by a non-Pentecostal group that wanted to learn more about spiritual warfare. This class helped me to realize that at one point in the life of these believers, they either had a personal "encounter" with the Spirit and the supernatural, or they knew of a friend that had that encounter. This class served to open up the conversation about the on-going work of the Holy Spirit in their lives without the fear of been judged.

As a result, I have included my own story of rejection and acceptance of the supernatural experiences of the Spirit in my spiritual journey. My goal has been to tell of my own personal experiences, then be able to articulate those experiences in ways that others might be able to relate or bring clarity to their own experiences.

Somebody has said, "Experience first, then comes the explanation of those experiences." This book relates personal accounts of the supernatural. It is also a survey of some contemporary writers who talk about these supernatural experiences, while at the same time the reader will find some scholarly resources that helps to solidify and give credibility to these experiences. I have used a variety of sources to challenge and expose the reader to new literature, new perspectives, and different traditions.

There are chapters that will be easy to read, others will require some deep thinking, but do not let that stop you. In the introduction, I define apocalyptic anointing. Chapter one relates my early experiences with the supernatural. Chapter two is about the role that the Spirit plays as a giver of spiritual gifts. There are different ways that the apocalyptic anointing is manifested, which chapter three begins to explore. Chapter four is about how to interpret and apply apocalyptic dreams and visions. Apocalyptic symbolism in warfare is chapters five. This chapter is about the on-going spiritual battle between God and Satan. Chapter six is about regional warfare, which I call Third-Level Spiritual warfare. The last chapter will help us to walk in the Spirit and to cultivate our spiritual growth in light of the on-going work of the Holy Spirit and the Word of God.

There is so much to learn about the apocalyptic anointing. Spiritual warfare and spiritual gifts are important for the church; however, there are many confusing views on these topics. My initial attempt is to give a new fresh perspective about the person and work of the Holy Spirit with regard to power, revelations, and spiritual warfare. Keep in mind the whole purpose of the gifts is that we grow closer to God and continue to deepen our love toward others.

Notes

1. Patricia King, *Spiritual Revolution: Experience the Supernatural in Your Life, Angelic Visitations, Prophetic Dreams, Visions and Miracles* (Shippensburg: Destiny Image, 2006), 36-37.

Introduction

In these end times, God is raising up people with a special anointing to unveil the forces of evil and to embrace God's warfare strategies. There is a need for God's people to receive the anointing from heaven in order to demolish the works of our enemy. God wants people who are serious about their calling and about serving him every day. God is seeking Christians who are willing to receive the apocalyptic anointing.

Defining the Apocalyptic Anointing

I am using the term "apocalyptic anointing" to describe the shocking revelations God gives to uncover the strategies of the enemy. This enables us to capture or perceive the spiritual settings that are currently affecting our world. The reason God gives spiritual insight into the supernatural world is so that those who have "eyes to see" may set individuals, churches, and regions free by the inhabiting power of the Holy Spirit. This anointing reveals the evil schemes that Satan and his Antichrist are planning for the world. When the unveiling of these satanic strategies happens, we can take the authority that Christ has given us to destroy the works of the devil. God unveils the enemy's strategies by giving prophetic or apocalyptic revelations. These revelations give us the insight to overcome the works of the enemy.

Unlike the prophetic voice that preaches (forth tells) or predicts the future (foretelling), the apocalyptic anointing reveals the actual work of Satan and God. It reveals the satanic works in nations and the rulers of the world. The fight that goes on hidden from our natural eyes between the forces of evil and the forces of God becomes apparent to the person who has this anointing. The apocalyptic anointing first gives discernment regarding what the enemy is doing against churches, regions, and/or nations in the spiritual realm, and then gives strategies to overcome his plan by allowing the kingdom of God and his angels to destroy his schemes.

The word 'anointing,' according to the dictionary, means, "to put oil in a religious ceremony as a sign of sanctification or consecration, and to choose by or as if by divine intervention."[1] *The Dictionary of Pentecostal and Charismatic Movements* speaks of the anointing with oil, "Anointing with oil also carried sacred or symbolic significance, indicated in the Old Testament (Hebrew word) *Masah*. Objects were anointed and consecrated to divine service (Exodus 30:26-29). Anointed persons received an infusion of divine presence and power, actualized for the Israelites by an endowment of the Spirit of Yahweh (1 Samuel 16:13)."[2] The anointed person is inhabited by the power and presence of God to do a specific assignment.

There are many books written on the anointing of the Spirit. In Kenneth E. Hagin's book, *Understanding the Anointing*,[3] he categorizes the anointing in three sections: the individual anointing, anointing on ministry gifts, and the corporate anointing. The anointing of ministry gifts brings the power of the Spirit according to the calling(s) of the particular individual's gifting. Therefore, the anointing of the prophet is different from the anointing to preach, the anointing of the apostle, or the anointing of the apocalyptist.

Robert H. Mounce in his textbook, *The Book of Revelation*, deals extensively with the definition of the word "apocalypse." He states, "the term apocalypse used to denote a literary genre is derived from Rev. 1:1, where it designates the supernatural unveiling of that which is about to take place."[4] Mounce also tackles the issue of the difference between a prophet and an apocalyptist, he states, "speaking generally, the prophets foretold the future that should arise out of the present, while the apocalyptists foretold the future that should break into the present."[5] Mounce mentions the method in which God talks to the seer, "The content of apocalyptic normally comes to the author by means of a dream or vision in which he is translated into heavenly realms where he is privileged to see revealed, the eternal secrets of God's purpose and such visions are held to have been given to ancient seers. The apocalyptist was a wise man uncovering the mysteries of God's purpose."[6]

Characteristics of the Apocalyptic Anointing

In scripture, the ultimate apocalyptic anointing is going to be manifested in the two witnesses (or as I like to call them, the two warriors) in Revelation 11. Revelation 11:3 and 6, states, "I will give power to my two witnesses, and they will prophesy...These men have the power to shut up the sky so that it will not rain during the time they are prophesying; and they have power to turn the waters into blood and to strike the earth with every kind of plague as often as they want" (NRSV). Since these two witnesses come from the presence of God, they fully carry the power and the anointing of God to accomplish his purposes. The anointing of the two witnesses is apocalyptic, prophetic, and powerful.

Clarence J. Abbott, in his paper, *Toward a Pentecostal Theology of Prophetic Witness: The Testimony of the Apocalypse* (Revelation 11:3-14), makes several important observations regarding how God gives apocalyptic revelation. Abbott's first observation is that the prophetic divine voice is speaking in first person—"I will give to my witnesses." [7] This indicates a close relationship between the apocalyptist and the divine speaker. God gives shocking revelations to those who thirst and hunger after his will.

Secondly, the apocalyptic anointing should be exercised within an apocalyptic community. Numbers 35:30 and Deuteronomy 17:6; 19:15 clarify that in order to validate truth you need two witnesses. There are no lone rangers with an apocalyptic witness—rather, there is the need for a community to validate and affirm the apocalyptist. At first, this apocalyptic community must discern the authenticities of the revelations that they are receiving, then the greater "Christian communities" must engage in the same process of discernment.

Third, the task of the apocalyptist is to prophesy to that which he/she witnesses, hears, and sees. Abbott writes, "The activity of these two witnesses is described as prophesying, a detail that emphasizes further the connection between witness and prophetic activity in the Apocalypse."[8]

Fourth, this task has a specific time for its fulfillment. Just like the two witnesses that will prophesy for 1,260 days, I believe that this is the time God is releasing His apocalyptic anointing upon those who are able to see and hear His divine plans. In these last days, God is anointing people for a specific ministry. This is the time where God is pouring out his Spirit—this is the season to capture and follow the call of God in order to do wonders for his glory!

Finally, the apocalyptist is a witness of the judgment that God brings upon the injustice and sin of those who do not repent. Abbott states, "The attire of these two witnesses, sackcloth, might well remind the hearers of the fact that in the Old Testament sackcloth was a sign of mourning (Is. 22:12; Jer 4:8; Jonah 3:6-8)."[9] Apocalyptists carry a heavy burden as they testify to the destruction that is to come.

From the example of the two witnesses, apocalyptic anointing is nurtured in intimacy with God and community. It is able both to participate with and speak God's will during a specific season to call sinners to repentance and to expose the enemy.

The apocalyptist uncovers the works of evil in spiritual settings and is able to see the work of God and his holy angels. God continues to use visions and dreams to communicate with contemporary apocalyptists. The way we see God and Satan at work is by the Spirit. The Holy Spirit is able to reveal "spiritual intelligence" of what God is up to and what the enemy is doing. Spiritual information about the spiritual realm is the key to seeing what God is doing and uncovering the evil plans Satan and his army are preparing against the world.

Keep in mind that there are two worlds in conflict. There is the physical world, and there is the spiritual world. God and Satan are in the spiritual realm. The apocalyptist understands that there are spiritual and earthly laws, and when those work in conjunction, things happen.

God is bringing together people who carry a unique anointing in their lives. Mary K. Baxter in her first book, *A Divine Revelation of Hell*, shares a prophecy, "Behold, I am preparing a holy army. They will do mighty exploits for me and destroy your high places. They are an army of holy men and women, boys and girls. In the past they have been misunderstood and mistreated, abused and rejected."[10] In the same prophecy, the Lord tells Mary that God is going to give gifts to this army to awaken many people to the truth and combat the evil and demonic forces in this world. Mary sees this army as the same army mentioned in the book of Joel. I believe that this end time army will embrace the apocalyptic anointing as they understand the call of God.

Notes

1. Modern Language Association (MLA): "anointing." *The American Heritage® Dictionary of the English Language*, Fourth Edition (Houghton Mifflin Company, 2004. 19 Jul. 200). <Dictionary.com http://dictionary.reference.com/browse/anointing>.

2. Burgess, Stanley and McGee, Gary. *Dictionary of Pentecostal and Charismatic Movements* (Grand Rapids: Zondervan Publishing, 1992), 11.

3. Hagin, E. Kenneth. *Understanding the Anointing* (Tulsa: Rhema Bible Church, 2004).

4. Mounce H. Robert, *The Book of Revelation* (Grand Rapids: Eerdmans Publishing, 1998), 1.

5. Ibid, 3.

6. Ibid, 4.

7. Claren Abbott, *Toward a Pentecostal Theology of Prophetic Witness: The Testimony of the Apocalypse (Revelation 11:3-14)*. Presented at the 36th Annual Meeting of the Society for Pentecostal Studies, 2007. 1.

8. Ibid, 2.

9. Ibid, 2.

10. Mary Baxter, *A Divine Revelation of Hell* (Springdale: Whitaker House, 1993), 140.

1

The Call of God

When I was in my preteens, I became very ill. While I was suffering from chicken pox, high fever, and serious dehydration, my mother invited two Assemblies of God Hispanic pastors to come pray for me. As these two pastors prayed for me, I gave my life to Jesus, and he healed me from my sickness. This Hispanic Assemblies of God church in Canada believed in the movement of the Spirit and his diverse gifts.

As I began to get serious about my faith, I fasted and prayed. I recall that before my pastor baptized me, he sat down with me and told me that there was another baptism—the baptism of the Holy Spirit. He asked me if he could lay hands on me to receive the baptism of the Holy Spirit. I remember his saying, "You might feel something or you might not, but seek it and the Lord will give it to you." He prayed for me and nothing happened. Then several days later, on my way to school, I began to speak in tongues.

The Visions Begin

This baptism awoke a hunger within my spirit. I began to fast and pray for God to move in the church. As I was seeking his face, I had two visions. When I closed my eyes in prayer, I saw the blue sky. In the sky, I saw a black circle hanging between the sky and earth. This first vision scared me because I had never seen into the spirit realm before. The next day I was in prayer again, and the Lord showed the same vision except that this time the black circle became a black liquid that was coming down to earth. This really disturbed me. Since I was new with visions, I went to my pastor to find out what was going on with all that I had seen.

After I explained the visions in detail, my pastor smiled and said, "The Lord is showing you a revelation that takes years for other Christians to see and/or receive. God is revealing these things to you at a fast pace." He then opened his Bible to Matthew 24:29, where Jesus says, "Immediately after the suffering of those days the sun will be darkened, and the moon will not give its light; the stars will fall from heaven, and *the powers of heaven will be shaken*" (NRSV, emphasis mine). My pastor explained to me that this text has meaning beyond the actual stars and heavens; it is also talking about the demonic powers that are in the heavenlies. Greg Boyd affirms, "Indeed, as a number of scholars have suggested, read in the light of the broader apocalyptic tradition, 'the stars' falling down from heaven and 'the powers in the heavens' being shaken (V. 29) may refer to rebel cosmic powers being defeated in battle."[1] In the last days, those powers are going to be shaken by the power of God. My pastor concluded, "Rony, God wants you to know who your enemy is." This was my first lesson in spiritual warfare and interpreting visions.

Encountering Darkness

In order to consider how the satanic powers in the heavens are operating, I will share one unforgettable experience that I had with the powers of darkness. One night I was sleeping, when all of a sudden I felt a force that was coming from outside the window trying to pull my spirit away from my body. I tried to wake up, but I could not. I knew what was going on—there was a demonic force in my room. As this demonic force was manifesting, I saw three human spirits—they were old with white hair and white beards. They were on top of my bed talking to each other trying to figure out what they were going to do with me. Finally, they decided to lay hands on me and they began to speak in a tongue that I could not understand.[2] As they prayed for me, I thought I was going to die. I felt that I could not wake up from my sleep.

Immediately, I saw a vision of a preacher saying, "Whatever you bind in heaven, you bind on earth. Whatever is loose in heaven is loose on earth." Then I felt the presence of God, and I began to rebuke those human spirits. After I rebuked them, they left, and I was able to wake up. I felt exhausted, as if I had run a marathon. It scared the living daylights out of me. Later on, I found out that the city I was living in, at that time, had two underground satanic churches. There were suspicions that these satanic churches were doing animal and human sacrifices. I believe that it was the leaders of the satanic church who came against me because of my new faith and God's call on my life. All these things happened to me when I was about 12 years old.

Even though I was young, I began to read on the subject of spiritual warfare. I wanted to make sense of my experiences. The first two books that I read were *A Divine Revelation of Hell*, by Mary Baxter and Rebecca Brown's book, *He Came to Set the Captives Free*. In a chapter entitled, "War in the Heavens," Mary Baxter talks about the dark spiritual circles associated with witchcraft. In an open vision, God revealed to Baxter those dark circles and what the circles represent.

Mary Baxter describes this open vision: "I saw a spiritual circle high above the earth. The circle was invisible to the natural eye, but in the spirit, I could see it well. I knew that the vision was related to our fight against the princes and powers of the air."[3] In fact, she sees more circles. From one of the circles she saw, "that a demon had arisen, and he was doing evil to the earth. The demon had the spirit of a wizard. He would turn and laugh, and from a stick in his hand, he cast evil spells on various people. I saw other evil spirits join the wizard, and Satan gave him more power."[4] I could not believe what I was reading. What she saw was similar to the two visions that I had had, and it was also wizards who tried to kill me.

This is how I was "baptized" into spiritual warfare. I knew that God was giving me a spiritual gift to see into the spiritual realm, but my pastor reminded me that I was not a special Christian. God desires all his people to utilize his gifts for his glory and to overcome the forces of evil. Although I understood this, I did not like it. It scared me very much. I knew what the power of God was capable of, and I was becoming aware of the power of darkness. I did not want to mess with either the power of God or the power of darkness. I knew the things I was seeing were out of this world. I wanted to be accepted and loved, but who would believe what I had seen in the spiritual realm? Deep in my heart, I also knew that God was calling me into the ministry. As I grew older, this gift was on the backburner. During college and seminary, I began to pay attention to it, but still was not interested in going back and revisiting my early spiritual experiences. It was not until I began pastoring that it became evident to me that this was an authentic gift and calling of God upon my life.

Diversity of the Calling

There are several callings in the Old Testament such as prophetic callings, priestly callings, and specific callings to assignments (e.g. judges). In the New Testament, some were called pastors, prophets, teachers, evangelists, and apostles. They all had unique gifts and anointing to fulfill their callings.

The new generation taking leadership roles in churches and other Christian organizations are not the traditional leaders of the past. They are gifted differently. The apocalyptic calling of God requires many different spiritual gifts. Some of them do not fit within traditional churches and denominations. The God that we serve is a creative God; he is always emphasizing or "calling forth" something new.

Called to the Apocalyptic Anointing

Throughout the years, I continued to have dreams and visions but I did not know what to call these experiences. The dominant theme of these dreams and visions was the cosmic fight between God and Satan. Unsure and even scared at times, I continued to seek God for an explanation of this phenomenon.

As I meditated upon a dream I had, these two words came into my spirit: apocalyptic anointing. I was shocked! I have always been an avid reader of prophetic and apocalyptic literature. But to put apocalyptic and anointing together was new to me. All of a sudden, the hours that I had spent reading and writing about these experiences came together. I began to study and define the apocalyptic anointing in the context of my life, in the context of biblical characters, in the context of historical figures, and in the context of the life of the church. I had seen pieces of the picture of my calling here and there, but now I was able to see the big picture.

Defining the Apocalyptic Anointing

The apocalyptic anointing gives shocking revelations to uncover the strategies of the enemy and sets individuals, churches, and regions free by the inhabiting power of the Holy Spirit. This God-given call and ability enables us to capture or perceive the spiritual settings that are currently affecting our world. The apocalyptic anointing is not just for the benefit of individuals; it impacts churches and whole regions as well because churches and regions are connected and cannot be separated. In the same way, the enemy has sent his powers to stop the work of Christ from flourishing. The apocalyptic anointing is for spiritual warfare. As God reveals spiritual strategy, the apocalyptist interacts with the spiritual realm in obedience to God's will. The apocalyptic anointing opens the eyes of the spirit to distinguish what is of God, what is of the flesh, and what is of Satan.

Biblical Examples

Daniel, Elijah, Zechariah, Ezekiel, John the Baptist, and John the Revelator had apocalyptic experiences and the ability to see visions. Let us consider several of these characters as we establish a biblical foundation for the apocalyptic anointing.

Daniel

Daniel had revelations from God because of his humble heart (Daniel 7). God sent an angel to fight the satanic principality who was opposing the message of God coming to Daniel. People who have the apocalyptic anointing are like Daniel who was able to influence kingdoms, empires, kings, and presidents for the kingdom of God.

The call in Daniel's life was extraordinary. Daniel 1:17, states, "to these four young men God gave knowledge and understanding of all kinds of literature and learning. And Daniel could understand visions and dreams of all kinds" (NIV). The gift of understanding visions and dreams was a gift given by God to Daniel. The Hebrew prophet Joel prophesied that in the last days, God was going to pour out his Spirit on all flesh, and they would prophesy and have dreams and visions. Dreams and visions are inspired by God to reveal his will and purpose. People have dreams and visions in different degrees; however when the apocalyptic anointing is active, dreams and visions contain clear and deep revelations of God. Chapters 7-12 of Daniel have some amazing visions and dreams declaring the purposes of God to different kingdoms of Daniel's time.

Elijah and John the Baptist

Elijah also had the power to affect the kingdom of Israel. The miraculous demonstration of the power of God in his life and ministry were evidence that God wanted Israel to turn back to him. The Elijah anointing had power to stop rain, call down fire from heaven, and part the Jordan River (1 Kings 17-2 Kings 2). These miracles captured the nation's attention.

Elijah is apocalyptic in that he confronted the spiritual oppression against the nation of Israel. He entered directly into a power encounter with the priest of Baal, King Ahab, and Jezebel. God transported him and hid him from King Ahab (1 Kings 18). Elijah stopped the rain, and then he prayed for rain to fall. After he met King Ahab on Mount Carmel, he was supernaturally empowered by God and ran faster than Ahab rode to beat the rain (1 Kings 18:46). The apocalyptic anointing gives us supernatural ability to see into the spiritual realm, and supernatural strength both physically and spiritually to combat the forces of evil. Spiritual warfare requires both physical and emotional energy, but God will supernaturally sustain his apocalyptists.

The apocalyptic anointing contains great power and shocking revelation. John and Paula Sandford elaborate on the spirit and power of Elijah in *The Elijah Task*.[5] They identify two aspects of Elijah's ministry. First, the spirit of Elijah offended the mind to reveal the heart. In other words, the Elijah spirit is all about repentance. Second, Elijah's ministry was marked by signs and wonders.

Revealing the Heart

First, the Sandfords recognize that this same spirit of Elijah was in John the Baptist: "John's inner garment is the garment of continuous piercing, pricking of the conscience, exposing every deception. We build the sort of self-congratulatory walls of pride and self-righteousness which John the Baptist opposed, and which God would hew down for all righteousness are as filthy rags (Isa. 64:6)."[6] The one who carries this apocalyptic anointing will do in part what the spirit of Elijah did: call people to repentance. The anointing reveals the identity of who we are. It exposes us, the real us. We are undone, and there is nothing left to do but repent. Once the anointing reveals your own heart, God will use you to uncover others' intrinsic motivations and true nature.

There have been occasions when God has given me sermons to challenge and rebuke certain congregations. My reaction is, "Lord, not again!" Certainly, I am fully aware that some people are going to get mad at me. Therefore, I am faced with a choice of whether or not I should preach that sermon. Furthermore, how am I going to articulate and convey the message to them? When God is ready to reveal the heart of his people, it is not easy for the messenger, nor is it easy for the congregation. All sins are revealed. If real transformation needs to happen, the heart must be revealed. When people repent, they come into alignment with God, and Satan's strongholds are broken.

As with the prophet Ezekiel when the glory of the Lord was in the temple, God revealed to him in depth the different types of hidden sins of the leaders of Israel (Ezekiel 8). The prophet was transported in visions from the land of the Babylonians to the temple of the Lord in Israel. From idolatry worship to demonic worship, God reveals in a very concise manner the sins the people were committing in the temple.

Signs and Wonders

Second, the power of Elijah included signs, wonders, miracles, and great revelations. The New Testament prophet who carried this apocalyptic anointing is different from the Old Testament prophets. Sandford states, "The prophet of the New Testament is not the miracle worker, not the healer, not the teacher, not the evangelist…the prophet is the enabler, the spark plug who gets others going. John's work was largely hidden, and wrestling in the desert with the unseen phantasmagoria of men's heart. John's work was done in fasting and hidden that others might shine when Jesus came."[7] The power of God is still as authentic and real as it was during the days of Elijah. But John was different. He prepared the way through spiritual warfare. The one who carries the apocalyptic anointing first needs to interact with the spiritual realm and win the hidden spiritual battle against the forces of evil and the sin that is enslaving men's hearts.

Those who carry the apocalyptic anointing have an experience similar to the U.S. Army units called Special Forces—each unit has four members, and each of the members has his or her own specialty. These Special Forces can be deployed anywhere in the world within a few hours to infiltrate the enemy's camp. Their battles are not made public. They do not get the public recognition they deserve, but this does not mean they are not engaged in battles around the world. Most of the time, those who have the calling to do spiritual warfare will not get the recognition that they deserve publicly in the church. However, this does not mean they are not engaged in a fight with the forces of evil in the spiritual realm.

John the Revelator

John was able to influence the Roman Empire and encouraged the Christians who had been persecuted by the early Roman emperors. Revelation 1:1 says, "The revelation of Jesus Christ, which God gave him to show his servants what must soon take place. He made it known by sending his angel to his servant John" (NIV). Again, we see that Christ gave this apocalyptic vision and utilized his angel to reveal it to John. In the Scriptures God is the author of dreams and visions; through them, he desires to communicate his will to us and communicate what the enemy is doing.

John, in his apocalyptic visions, was able to interact with the supernatural. Unlike the spirit and power of Elijah that revealed men's hearts, John interacted with the spiritual realm where God and Satan are engaged in a cosmic battle. John was not just a spectator to the visions that he saw; he participated in the spiritual realm by interacting with the angels of heaven. For instance, in chapter five in the scene of the scroll and the lamb, no one was able to break the seals and open the scroll. At this point, John began to cry. Nevertheless, one of the elders told him not to cry, because the only one who was able to break and open the scroll is Jesus (Revelations 5:5). One last example is found in Revelation 17:6-8. Here John was astonished when he saw the prostitute of Babylon, and the Angel asked him, "Why are you astonished?" So we see that John did not just experience supernatural empowering, he interacted with the supernatural in his visions.

The prophet Ezekiel had a similar experience when God asked him to eat the scroll. In Ezekiel 2:9-3:1-4, we discover how he interacted with the supernatural realm:

> Then I looked, and I saw a hand stretched out to me. In it was a scroll, which he unrolled before me. On both sides of it were written words of lament and mourning and woe. And he said to me, "Son of man, eat what is before you, eat this scroll; then go and speak to the house of Israel." So I opened my mouth, and he gave me the scroll to eat. Then he said to me, "Son of man, eat this scroll I am giving you and fill your stomach with it." So I ate it, and it tasted as sweet as honey in my mouth. He then said to me: "Son of man, go now to the house of Israel and speak my words to them." (NIV)

The interaction between the prophet and God by eating the scroll is about being obedient to speak God's word.

The prophetic anointing challenges God's people to understand that, if they are not obedient to his word, there are consequences for their actions. It is about calling people to repentance. When God's people do not repent, the message no longer becomes a message of repentance but one of judgment. The apocalyptic anointing breaks into the present; the judgment is imminent. The people have already made their choice, but even as they suffer the consequences, God extends his forgiveness.[8] Clearly, scripture is full of examples of the apocalyptic anointing in action. It is not, however, the only source of information on this unique anointing. Plenty of examples can be found in post-biblical history as well.

St Anthony

One of the monks of early Christian history was St. Anthony. *Turning Points: Decisive Moments in the History of Christianity*, by Mark A. Noll, says of Anthony, "The first monks, like Anthony, who left Egyptian cities for the desert, were thus departing from a world where both spiritual and secular conditions lay in disarray."[9] There were many motives for monks who went and lived their separated spiritual lives. For instance, St. Anthony, after hearing a sermon on Matthew 19:21, gave to the villagers about three hundred acres that were left to him from his parents. During this time, these monks made a difference by saving the spiritual life of the church.

Alister E. McGrath, in his book, *Christian Literature*, described St. Anthony's spiritual warfare with several demons. McGrath says, "But changes of form for evil are easy for the devil, so in the night they made such a din that the whole of that place seemed to be shaken by an earthquake, and the demons as if breaking the four walls of the dwelling seem to enter through them, coming in the likeness of beasts and creeping things. And the place was on a sudden filled with the forms of lions, bears, leopards, bulls, serpents, asps, scorpions, and wolves, and each of them was moving according to his nature."[10] This is an example of how various demons manifested as different animals while he prayed. St. Anthony saw the demons that were attacking him in the spiritual realm. Likewise, God is able to reveal the darkness that comes against us. These demonic forces come to destroy our lives, our finances, our families and our churches. When we pray we push darkness away and experience freedom in these areas. He also did spiritual warfare against the demons of sickness. St. Anthony confronted the demons' authority, and he found out that the demons and all their manifestations did not have power over him. After resisting the demons, his pain swiftly left and the building returned to its normal state.

In the apocalyptic anointing, one is able to move away from the things of the world into the things of the spirit. Most Christians think that not entangling themselves with the things of the world is their only duty in their religious practice. In the life of St. Anthony, we learn that just moving from the world and selling our possessions is not enough. There is a spiritual world that we need to fight against, and it is in the power and the anointing of the Spirit that we conquer these forces.

St. Patrick

St. Patrick was the missionary who initially introduced Christianity to the Irish. His ministry to them was initiated by a vision. After living as a captive for six years in Ireland, St. Patrick returned to his home country, only to have God ask him to go back to those who held him captive. He wrote about a vision where he "...saw a man coming, as it were from Ireland. His name was Victoricus, and he carried many letters, and he gave me one of them. I read the heading: 'The Voice of the Irish'. As I began the letter, I imagined in that moment that I heard the voice of those very people who were near the wood of Foclut, which is beside the western sea—and they cried out, as with one voice: 'We appeal to you, holy servant boy, to come and walk among us.'"[11]

There can be no doubt that St. Patrick had supernatural experiences from God. He also had a guardian angel that inspired him to fast and pray on a mountain. The Catholic Encyclopedia explains, "The whole purpose of his prayer was to obtain special blessings and mercy for the Irish race, whom he evangelized. The demons that made Ireland their battlefield mustered all their strength to tempt the saint and disturb him in his solitude, and turn him away, if possible, from his pious purpose. They gathered around the hill in the form of vast flocks of hideous birds of prey. So dense were their ranks that they seemed to cover the whole mountain, like a cloud, and they so filled the air that Patrick could see neither sky nor earth nor ocean. St. Patrick besought God to scatter the demons, but for a time it would seem as if his prayers and tears were in vain."[12] This is an example of spiritual warfare for the souls of the Irish and for the country of Ireland. The biblical and historical examples help us to understand and embrace this anointing.

It is clear at this point that the apocalyptic anointing is about a greater depth of revelation and has a great power to destroy the forces of darkness. The biblical examples of Daniel, Elijah, John the Baptist, and John the Revelator demonstrate deep insights into the spiritual world as well as the power that comes along with those revelations to overcome the forces of evil.

The historical accounts of St. Anthony and St. Patrick solidify the fact that this spiritual warfare is an eternal battle. Christians in the past have fought this battle, and God is seeking new warriors to enlist in this current fight. My personal experience of this fight affirms in me that he continues to bestow the apocalyptic anointing to those who respond to his calling. The Spirit is poured out upon all flesh, and those who respond to his Spirit are able to fight this cosmic battle.

Notes

1. Boyd, Gregory. *God at War* (Downers Grove: Intervarsity Press, 1997), 227.
2. Astral projection occurs when witches or warlocks get out of their physical bodies with the help of demons and travel in their spirits to do spiritual or physical damage to some one. See *Prepare for War* by Rebecca Brown.
3. Baxter, Mary, *A Divine Revelation of Hell* (Springdale: Whitaker House, 1993), 157-158.
4. Ibid 158.
5. Sanford, John and Paula. *The Elijah Task* (Tulsa: Victory House, 1977).
6. Ibid 10.
7. Ibid 18.
8. Revelation 9:20-21
9. Noll, A. Mark, *Turning Points: Decisive Moments in the History of Christianity* (Grand Rapids: Baker Academic, 2000), 88.
10. McGrath, Alister. *Christian Literature: An Anthology* (Malden: Blackwell Publishers Ltd, 2001), 73.
11. http://en.wikepedia.org/wiki/Saint_Patrick
12. http://www.newadvent.org/cathen/11554a.htm

2

Apocalyptic Pneumatology

My freshman year in Bible college I wrote an essay about the experiences and encounters that I had with the Holy Spirit. My New Testament professor read it and said, "You better look at pneumatology in order to bring a valid claim to your experiences." This was a big word for a freshman in Bible college! *Pneuma*, like the Old Testament word *ruach*, has the basic meaning of air and breathing. Often this word is translated in the Bible as Spirit. Therefore *Pneuma* is Spirit, and *ology* is study—the study of the Holy Spirit.

As I studied the person and work of the Spirit, my findings brought validity to how God was working in my life. I was better able to distinguish what the Holy Spirit was doing. I came to understand in a new way that the intense visions and experiences that I had all originated in the Spirit. The Holy Spirit is the source of the apocalyptic anointing. As we study who he is and how he works, we will be able to articulate our experiences to the broader Christian community. Study in this way may be a challenge, but it is this intellectual study that will ground you.

As I broadened my study of the Holy Spirit, I was surprised by the insights of those with different Christian traditions. Having only been exposed to Pentecostal and charismatic believers, the witness and perspective of those outside these groups enabled me to appreciate new and different aspects of the Holy Spirit's work and gifts. As we unpack the Holy Spirit's work related to the apocalyptic anointing, I will draw from a variety of different traditions.

Pneumatology

Typically, theology books divide pneumatology into two main sections. First they look at the person of the Holy Spirit, and then the work of the

Holy Spirit. This is the case of Millard J. Erickson's, *Christian Theology*, which reiterates these three reasons why the study of the Spirit is important in our culture today and adds another. For our purposes, let me state this third reason. Erickson says, "...the importance of the doctrine of the Holy Spirit is that our current culture stresses the experiential, and it is primarily through the Holy Spirit's work that we feel God's presence within and the Christian life is given a special tangibility."[1] Erickson, a Baptist theologian, emphasizes the importance of the subjective role of the Spirit. We need to broaden and deepen our intellectual study of the Holy Spirit to bring affirmation to our personal experiences and to reach out to those seeking encounters with the supernatural. As our culture is open to a variety of "experiences," Christians must be able to understand, discuss, and discern how the Holy Spirit is at work. The apocalyptic anointing flows through these experiences. It is vital that we have sound pneumatology that is objectively grounded in the word of God and the community of faith, yet remains open to the subjective, ongoing revelations and work of the Spirit.

Pentecostals and charismatics recognize the Spirit in every facet of the Christian life. For example, in *Rites in the Spirit: A Ritual Approach to Pentecostal/Charismatic Spirituality*, Daniel Albrecht defines Pentecostal and charismatic spirituality "as a particular configuration of beliefs, practices and sensibilities that put the believer in an on-going relationship to the Spirit of God."[2] This on-going relationship with the Spirit of God is further developed in the Pentecostal/Charismatic worship style. This "worship involves a deep communion between divinity and humanity, an encountering, a mutual experience...the Spirit initiates, guides, facilitates, and leads the worship."[3] During times of worship the Spirit of God is free to speak to us individually and bring specific revelation. As we abide in an ongoing relationship with the Holy Spirit, we will encounter him throughout our day and when we least expect it.

The Person of the Holy Spirit

The Spirit is God. Theologians call this the deity of the Holy Spirit. Acts 5:3-4 solidifies the fact that the Spirit is God. Peter asked, "Ananias, how is it that Satan has so filled your heart that you lied to the Holy Spirit and have kept for yourself some of the money you received for the land? You have not lied to men but to God." In 1 Corinthians 3:16-17, Paul writes, "Do you not know that you yourselves are God's temple and that God's Spirit lives in you?" John 4:24 states, "God is Spirit, and his worshipers must worship in spirit and in truth." These and other scriptures establish that the Spirit is God.

Erickson states with regard to the personality of the Spirit, "The Bible makes clear in several ways that the Holy Spirit is a person and possesses all the qualities which that implies."[4] First, He is the Spirit of truth (John 16:13) and a person who tells the truth. The Spirit is the comforter (*parakletos*)—he comforts believers (John 14:26). The Spirit is in relationship with the Father and the Son (Matthew 3:16-17). Finally, Erickson says, "The Holy Spirit engages in moral actions and ministries that can be performed only by a person. Among these activities are teaching, regenerating, searching, speaking, interceding, commanding, testifying, guiding, illuminating, revealing."[5]

The Work of the Holy Spirit

The Holy Spirit is active in many ways: in creation, in convicting of sin, in bringing judgment, and in blessing believers with spiritual gifts. The work of the Holy Spirit is evident in both the Old Testament and New Testament. In the New Testament, the work of the Holy Spirit is carefully studied in the life of Jesus, in the life of the Christian, and through the gifts of the Holy Spirit. The work of the Holy Spirit in the Christian life manifests the gifts of the Holy Spirit. Erickson says, "The Spirit also bestows certain special gifts on believers within the body of Christ."[6] Baptist Charismatic theologian, Clark H. Pinnock, in his book *Flame of Love: A Theology of the Holy Spirit*, encourages an openness to let the gifts of the Holy Spirit move in the local congregations. Pinnock says, "The Spirit is present beyond liturgy in a wider circle. There is a flowing that manifests itself as power to bear witness, heal the sick, prophesy, praise God enthusiastically, perform miracles and more. There is a liberty to celebrate, an ability to dream and see visions, a release of Easter life."[7] It is imperative that the Spirit be free to move in our worship services regardless of style.

When the gifts of the Spirit manifest, we enter into the spiritual realm, a realm that is subjective for many people. We must have both spiritual experiences and theological articulation—in other words, we must develop words and understanding to convey our experiences to others. It is difficult to explain theologically the manifestations of the Spirit. Veli-Matti Karkkainen, in his book *Pneumatology: The Holy Spirit in Ecumenical, International, and Contextual Perspective*, expounds on the dichotomy that exists between "personal principle" and "institutional principle." Veli-

Matti says, "The 'personal principle' refers to the place accorded to the initiatives of individuals as persons and to what those persons have to say on the basis of personal convictions. The 'institutional principle' sees the church as a communion of such persons led by the Spirit. A healthy pneumatology requires balance between these two seemingly contradictory orientations."[8] The individual's experiences have to be discerned within a community setting. First comes the supernatural experiences of the Spirit then comes theological articulation. Veli-Matti states, "This is clearly evident in the biblical record: a powerful, often charismatic experience of the Spirit came first; only afterward, and in a slow tempo, came theological reflection."[9] Reflection comes after the gifts of the Spirit manifest in our lives.

The Gifts of the Spirit

The word *gift* has several different meanings in the New Testament. Clark notices, "The term gift or charism has a spectrum of biblical meanings. It may refer to the gift of salvation (Rom 6:23), some benefit communicated through one's life (Rom 1:11) or a specific ability such as speaking in other tongues (1 Cor 13:1). The word is related etymologically to grace (*charis*) and points to the gracious workings of God."[10] These varied meanings of the term *charisma* create tension among the different circles of Christianity. Everyone has a different perspective on the gifts of the Spirit.

Benny C. Aker, in his journal article "Charismata: Gifts, Enablements, or Ministries?," explains that there are several problems in understanding the proper meaning of the term *gift*. He specifically concentrates on overcoming the exegetical and linguistic fallacies of the word charisma. For instance, he summarizes the usage of the word *charisma* in the book of Romans as 1) The whole plan of salvation (Romans 5:15-16), 2) Eternal life (Romans 6:23), 3) God's plan for Israel, and 4) Spiritual gifts (Romans 1:1; 11:29 and 12:6).[11] Although there is great diversity in the meaning and usage of the word *charisma*, most theologians focus on *charism* as spiritual gifts. However, these gifts may be categorized differently.

Millard Erickson lists the gifts found in four different New Testament books. Romans 12:6-8 contains prophecy, service, teaching, exhortation, liberality, giving aid, and acts of mercy. 1 Corinthians 12:4-11 includes wisdom, knowledge, faith, healing, working of miracles, prophecy, ability to distinguish spirits, various tongues, and interpretation of tongues.

Ephesians 4:11 lists apostles, prophets, evangelists, pastors and teachers. Aker mentions Berding's categorization of the gifts, which is Berding proposes, "to replace 'spiritual gifts' to the general word ministries."[12] In the case of the gifts in Ephesians 4:11, this makes sense—it seems that the five-fold offices are directly connected to the spiritual gifts. The five ministries are called gifts or "ascension gifts" (Ephesians 4:8). Personally, I am uncomfortable with the distinction that some try to make between spiritual gifts and ministry gifts, but I believe that ministries are gifts of the Spirit. The last passage, 1 Peter 4:11, contains the gifts of speaking and service.[13]

Embracing the Gifts

It is common for those who have spiritual gifts to initially be afraid of them. The key is that they overcome the initial fears and seek to understand their gifts intellectually and intuitively. Dr. David Ireland, in his book *Activating the Gifts of the Holy Spirit*, explains five enemies of spiritual gifts. The enemies are fear: of the supernatural, fear of not being socially accepted, lack of the carnal mind's understanding the desire for control, and the lack of discernment.

The first enemy is fear of supernatural experiences. Ireland states, "The tendency of human nature is to avoid things that are mysterious or beyond rational explanation. For this reason, most Christians approach the subject of the supernatural with much trepidation. No one is afraid of a Bible study on the topic. But a personal challenge to be used by God in the realm of the supernatural would make most people very apprehensive."[14]

This fear of the supernatural is one that I have had to struggle with since my initial spiritual experiences. The supernatural is a realm of which I was not aware. One day God decided to give me a vision of the supernatural, and I almost fell out of my bed! Now I understand why God opened my eyes to the supernatural. He wanted me to see who my spiritual enemy is. Because I was perplexed and even confused, I am glad that God put in my path a spiritually savvy pastor who helped me make sense of these supernatural experiences.

The second enemy of spiritual gifts is fear of social acceptance. Ireland says, "Throughout church history, the gifts of the Spirit have been avoided by well-intentioned saints who were unable to detect the invisible war between social acceptance and the supernatural."[15] Ireland goes on to give a personal example of how he grew up in a household that prided itself on being socially intelligent. One day, he recounts, the Lord sent him to prophesy to a church—he stood up in the pews and prophesied that the church should release the pastor to expand his ministry internationally. Everybody was astonished, including the worship leader because he did not know what to do. The pastor stood and said he did not know him, but that what he said was true. Ireland says, "Today the pastor has a powerful international ministry based out of that same local church I visited. The church graciously received the word and acted upon it."[16]

It is hard to be obedient when one is afraid of rejection. In high school, I moved to a new city. There I went to a church and high school that were primarily Anglo. My brothers and I were the only Hispanics in that area, and we were "novelties". I did not want to do anything or give anyone room not to like us because we were Hispanics. Although the church believed in the gifts of the Spirit, I did not want to stick out by using my spiritual gifts. So for many years, I did my best to neutralize the intense spiritual gifts I experienced as a new Christian.

Enemies number three and four go together: the carnal mind and control. Ireland states regarding the carnal mind, "The logic of the Spirit and how he manifests himself in the church through his gifts is not according to our way of thinking. His ways are higher than our ways, and his thoughts are higher than our thoughts."[17] However, the logical person thinks that our theology, philosophy, and our science override God's thoughts. When these things override God's word, there is room for control. "The desire to control the form of worship and the way faith is practiced causes some people to make terrible mistakes in spiritual discernment and in the theology they concoct to support their faulty perception,"[18] Ireland says.

Another enemy of spiritual gifts is the lack of discernment. There are many proponents of spirituality in our culture who are not Christian but pagan in origin. Many Christians run into this New Age spirituality because of their lack of discernment. The purpose for discernment "has been provided to the church by God to ensure our health and purity."[19] The way that one can win against these enemies is by feeding one's faith—"the enemies of the gifts will be starved into submission."[20]

I continued to try to make sense of and accept my spiritual gifts—especially the gift of spiritual warfare. I went to a Pentecostal university in hopes of learning more about spiritual warfare, but the information that I found was minimal. The one thing that I learned was how to balance the "intellectual" (mind) and the "heart" in order to be objective and subjective at the same time. To the natural eye, there is nothing fun about engaging the evil forces, but for the spiritual man it is an exciting event because you are able to participate in God's will.

Since it was neither fun nor exciting for my flesh, I struggled to follow my call. In the process of not following my call, I became unsatisfied. I tried to fill that void by doing other things in the ministry instead of following my call. Nothing satisfied me. I became unhappy and made my family and everybody else around me unhappy because of the emptiness in my heart. I wanted to do ministry my way, not God's way. God has graciously led me back into his calling and into his gifts.

One thing I learned while running away from my calling is the emptiness and hurt that one experiences for simply not embracing God's will, gifts, and anointing. This deeply hurt my relationship with God and my relationship with the people that I love the most. After this awful experience, I realized that there are people who are sitting in the pews of churches across the country with a mean and unhappy face because they have neglected to follow God's will in their calling. They are doing everything else, except for what God called them to do. I was there once, so I can relate.

In the midst of this inner conflict, I began to learn that God has created us in three parts. 1 Thessalonians 5:23, states, "May God himself, the God of peace, sanctify you through and through. May your whole spirit, soul, and body be kept blameless at the coming of our Lord Jesus Christ" (NIV). Without doing much hermeneutical and exegetical work in this passage, we can easily conclude that we are a trichonomy (three parts).[21] God works in each part. There is a classic work by Watchman Nee that does not receive much credit. His work, *The Spiritual Man*, may be considered practical theology and offers much in terms of how God works with our spirit, soul and body.

The emphasis of Nee's work is to move beyond our mind and physical body to relate to God in our spirit. It is in our spirits that God communes with us, and it is through the process of discernment that we come to understand and commune with God. Discernment is God's revelation about a particular situation or scenario.

Practical Guidelines

The Ecumenical Chronicle, which belongs to the World Church Council (WCC), published a statement from a WCC advisory group who met at Schloss Schwanberg on December 1978 on the topic of "Towards a

Church Renewed and United in the Spirit."[22] Section 5 *Gifts of the Spirit and Discernment: Some Practical Considerations* defines the purpose of the gifts of the Spirit. It says, "Spiritual gifts are specific forms of grace, which by their variety will reflect the fullness of the Spirit and the universality of grace."[23] Then the article goes on to give four practical guidelines for dealing with spiritual gifts. First, the gift is never a possession but remains dependent on the giver, which is the Holy Spirit. Second, the individual does not make his or her gift a measure for others, but the others become the measure for the exercise of the gift. Third, the delight over the visible appearance of the Spirit in specific experiences should not result in the trivialization of the Spirit but rather in the acknowledgement of his mystery. Fourth, all experiences of God's immediacy remain a mediated immediacy, meaning that the Spirit does not wish to work without or outside the given processes of nature and history. The recognition of these mediations (cultural, historical, social, psychological, etc.) cannot possibly imply any diminution but only the enrichment of our knowledge of God.[24] These practical guidelines are essential to keep a proper perspective of the work of the Holy Spirit. We should not judge others based upon our personal experiences. The Spirit calls people into ministry. People from various backgrounds respond to the call of God. We never encounter the supernatural in a vacuum; we need to consider all that God is doing through other people and other mediations.

There is a tendency to think that manifestations of spiritual gifts in a believer's life are a sign of maturity. The apocalyptic anointing is a gift, not a sign of maturity. When one receives revelations and visions it is easy to forget that these are gifts of grace. Rick Warren states that mature believers "have a servant's heart, and give freely out of maturity rather than giftedness."[25] Countless numbers of times we have seen gifted preachers fall into sin. Gifted people are not holier than thou! One has to grow in the spiritual gifts to reach maturity.

As we understand and develop our spiritual gift, we need to become more sensitive to the leading of the Holy Spirit in our lives. Jean-Pierre De Caussade in *The Sacrament of the Present Moment*, states, "It is the true voice of prophecy, an inner revelation, the doctrine of the Holy Spirit. In order to understand it, it is necessary to be in a state of total self-surrender, completely detached from every purpose and every interest, however holy, to have no interest in the world than passively submit to divine action in order to devote oneself to the duty of one's state, allowing the Holy Spirit to act in us regardless of what it is doing, happy, even, to remain in ignorance."[26] Many people do not understand how to hear and follow the Spirit—they try to control God or to be in control of their gifts.

Watchman Nee

The most comprehensive and complete work on how to understand our spirit, soul, and physical body is found in Watchman Nee's book entitled, *The Spiritual Man*.[27] To my knowledge, no other Christian writer has done a work like Watchman Nee's in terms of explaining biblically and theologically how God has created us. If you have not yet read his work, I would suggest that you pick up a copy. God uses Nee to introduce how one can enter into a loving relationship with God. The book is a combination of three volumes on the spiritual man. [See chart on the next page].

Although there is much to say about this book, I find the distinction he makes between the spirit and the soul to be very helpful. He teaches us how to know what is God's work in our spirit and what is our own emotion.

The Christian Led by the Soul

One of the ways that Christians follow their soul is by being impatient. Nee says, "Even in God's work, these Christians are so propelled by their zeal and passion that they simply cannot stay for God to make clear His will and way."[28] I remember that when God called me into the ministry I wanted God to make me a pastor of a large church and give me lots of money so I could do ministry right away. I did not have patience to wait for God's timing or discern his will for my ministry.

Another example Nee gives of how Christians can be impatient is when they get tired of having a pastor that has been around for ten or eighteen years. Some church leaders begin to create havoc in the congregation so the pastor will leave the church. The classic example is when the pastor does not follow the agenda of domineering leaders in the church—these leaders try to find faults in the pastor so they can oust her or him. These leaders claim that they are doing what is best for the church, and that they are hearing from God, when in reality they are merely soulish Christians.

The soul life in Christians is manifested on the one hand by self-styled wisdom with many opinions, and, on the other hand, by emotional sensations sought in spiritual experiences. Within evangelical and mainline churches there are many opinions about the Bible, ministry,

Outline of the Spiritual Man by Watchman Nee

Part One	Part Four	Part Eight
Volume 1	Volume 2	Volume 3
Introduction 1. Spirit, Soul, and Body 2. Spirit and Soul 3. The Fall of Man 4. Salvation	The Spirit 1. The Holy Spirit and the Believer's Spirit 2. A Spiritual Man 3. Spiritual Work 4. Prayer and Warfare	The Analysis of the Soul—the Mind 1. The Mind a Battlefield 2. The Phenomena of a Passive Mind 3. Way of Deliverance 4. The Laws of the Mind
Part Two The Flesh 1. Flesh and Salvation 2. Fleshly or Carnal Believer 3. Cross and Holy Spirit 4. Boastings of Flesh 5. Believers Ultimate Attitude towards the Flesh	Part Five An Analysis of the Spirit 1. Intuition 2. Communion 3. Conscience	Part Nine The Analysis of the Soul—the Will 1. A Believer's Will 2. Passivity and its Dangers 3. The Believer's Mistake 4. The Path to Freedom.
Part Three The Flesh 1. Deliverance from Sin Soul Life 2. The Experience of Soulish Believers 3. The Dangers of Soulish Life 4. The Cross and the Soul 5. Spiritual Believers and the Soul.	Part Six Walking after the Spirit 1. The Dangers of Spiritual Life 2. Laws of the Spirit 3. The Principle of Mind Aiding the Spirit 4. The Normalcy of the Spirit.	Part Ten The Body 1. The Believer and his Body 2. Sickness 3. God as the Life of the Body 4. Overcoming Death
	Part Seven The Analysis of the Soul—Emotion 1. The Believer and Emotion 2. Affection 3. Desire 4. A Life of Feeling 5. The Life of Faith	

and how we ought to do things. They are just opinions but they trump not only the needs and ideas of others but also the will of God. These individuals are led by their minds. I have also seen the other extremes where people are not led by their minds, but by theirs emotions. In Pentecostal and charismatic circles, sensations and emotions are given more credence than knowledge and logic. The latter are not accepted as being from God. Nee states, "Some incline more to the mind while others to emotion or will. Both, however, belong to the soul."[29] This is true within both the evangelical and Pentecostal/charismatic traditions.

Pentecostals and charismatics are accused of being too emotional, loud, and obnoxious. In their style of worship the music is loud and very expressive. Often they are neither reflective nor contemplative in church services.

Emotional expressions can lead evangelicals and other people to come to twisted and disturbing conclusions. I remember one time when I was talking to a non-Pentecostal Charismatic pastor about emotional experiences within the Pentecostal Charismatic experiences. This pastor told me without hesitation that the reason he went to a Pentecostal church when he was in the military was to meet girls. From an emotional perspective, according to this pastor, these Pentecostal girls work themselves up emotionally. Therefore, they were easily seduced by these military men. My jaw dropped when I heard what this pastor said. In fact, I was disturbed for several weeks that a person would think that of a Pentecostal charismatic worship service.

Worship can become soulish regardless of style. The traditional worshipers complain that contemporary music is too loud, and contemporary people complain that liturgical services are boring or dead—they judge each other's worship to be fleshy and distasteful to God. The worship of the soul can be intellectual and/or emotional; it reveals the heart. God wants us to worship and love him with both our intellect and emotions. True worshippers are transformed as they worship in spirit and truth.

Cultivating the Spirit

Nee recognized that many believers remain in the soul realm never understanding that they have a spirit. He states, "It is imperative that a believer knows he has a spirit, since, as we shall soon learn, every communication of God with man occurs there. If the believer does not discern his own spirit, he invariably is ignorant of how to commune with

God in the spirit. He easily substitutes the thoughts or emotions of the soul for the works of the spirit. Then he confines himself to the outer realm, unable ever to reach the spiritual realm."[30] Romans 8:16 supports this point: "It is the Spirit himself bearing witness with our spirit that we are children of God." One who has the apocalyptic anointing needs to know and relate to God in his spirit in order to discern what God is doing and what the enemy of our soul is planning against God's people.

There are three main organs of the spirit that need to be cultivated in order for the believer to see into the spiritual realm and fellowship with God. The first one is conscience. Conscience is "the discerning organ which distinguishes right or wrong; not, however, through the influence of knowledge stored in the mind but rather by a spontaneous direct judgment"(NIV)[31] One of the scriptures Nee gives in support of the function of conscience in man's spirit is, "His spirit was *provoked* within him as he saw that the city was full of idols" (Acts 17:16; see also 1 Corinthians 5:3; 2 Corinthians 2:3).

The second organ of the spirit is intuition. Intuition is the sensing organ of the human spirit. Nee states, "We really know through our intuition; our mind merely helps us to understand. The revelations of God and all the movements of the Holy Spirit are known to the believer through his intuition."[32] The function of intuition in man's spirit is supported by the following scriptures, "The spirit indeed is willing" (Matt. 26:41), and "What person knows a man's thought except the spirit of the man which is in him" (1 Corinthians 2:11).

The last organ to cultivate is worship. "Communion is worshiping God. The organs of the soul are incompetent to worship God. God is not apprehended by our thoughts, feelings or intentions, for He can only be known directly in our spirits,"[33] declares Watchman Nee. The function of communion in man's spirit is exemplified in Luke 1:47, "My spirit rejoices in God my savior" and "The true worshipers will worship the Father in spirit and truth" (John 4:23). True worship happens in the inner man—where God dwells and lives. Because God dwells there, the Holy Spirit can express his thoughts into our intuition.

The anointing of God rests on our intuition—Nee says, "The intuition of which we have been speaking is exactly the locus where occurs the anointing that teaches: you have been anointed by the Holy One, and you all know…"[34] (1 John 2:20). This anointing gives us spiritual discernment, guidance, and revelation. Revelation "has no other meaning than the Holy Spirit enables a believer to apprehend a particular matter by indicating the reality of it to his spirit."[35] The apocalyptic anointing increases spiritual insight in another dimension so we can capture what God is doing in his kingdom and in the kingdom of darkness.

I have been in church services where the presence and the anointing of the Holy Spirit comes upon the service. All of a sudden, there is a holy hush, and God begins to minister to people. Some see visions of how God is working in their church or in their lives. During this period of time, the intuition is open to grasp and see how the Spirit is moving and what he wants to accomplish. This is a moment when heaven invades earth, where God meets with his people. It can happen corporately or during personal times of prayer and worship. This type of worship goes beyond the intellect and emotions, because at that point we are not in control, but God is moving by his Spirit. During these experiences, there is an authentic awareness of the presence of the Holy Spirit; this is when we are open to the move of God, and God comes to fellowship and commune with us.

Pentecostal Perspective: Spirit Baptism

As mentioned earlier in chapter one, I came to know Christ within a Hispanic Assemblies of God church. At that time, my personal understanding of baptism of the Spirit was that the Spirit gives you power and love to minister to others. I became disillusioned with Pentecostalism as I observed how Pentecostals put great emphasis on the gifts but never on the fruit of the Spirit, especially love. There were many spiritual gifts manifesting in the churches I grew up in, but those gifts were being administered to others without love. Hence, many people were hurt by those very gifts that were given by God. To my knowledge, some of those people who were hurt have never come back to church.

This realization made me question many things about the work of the Spirit in the life of the believer. In some ways, I became bitter and resented the fact that people had the Spirit yet operated without love. Only recently have Pentecostal scholars begun to question the traditional view of the baptism of the Holy Spirit. The conversations have moved from defending the baptism of the Spirit and the initial evidence of speaking in tongues to accepting a more open view on the baptism of love. Obviously, ongoing conversation continues to revise our understanding of the baptism of the Holy Spirit despite the doctrinal close-mindedness that exists in terms of this issue.[36]

One Pentecostal scholar who brings a fresh perspective on the baptism of the spirit as the baptism of love is Frank Macchia. Chapter six of his book, *Baptized in the Spirit: A Global Pentecostal Theology* agrees that love should be the focus of living a spirit-filled life. He sees that the "Spirit baptism as the inauguration of the kingdom of God thus serves to integrate sanctification and charismatic gifting/empowerment."[37] The start of the spiritual encounters with God begins when one is baptized with love from heaven. The love releases the Spirit and his gifts to operate within the believer. This is when visions, dreams, and the gifts of God begin to operate. All of the gifts, including the apocalyptic anointing, need to flow out of the baptism of love.

"It is in the realm of the Spirit that I participate in the *koinonia* of divine love with others and discover my unique gifting as a channel of grace to others. It is in the realm of the Spirit that I join my heart with the one who so loves the world and sent the divine Son to seek and to save the lost,"[38] says Macchia. We cannot enter into the spiritual realm unless we have received his love, and that love motivates us to be in communion with God, often leading us to minister to others. It is not about us, but it is about ministering to others with compassion and love. This is contrary to the experiences and focus of many Pentecostals who strive for personal perfection and continue to focus on themselves. They seek the baptism of the Holy Spirit in a self-actualization effort.

Frank Macchia concludes this chapter by summarizing, "The Pentecostals ask us to experience a foretaste of that glory in the here and now as a force for renewal in the Christian life and the life of the church."[39] It is now, today, that we can be renewed by the glory of God. The transformation is for the now, for our everyday lives and ministry.

Different sources have been used in this chapter that shed light on the person and work of the Holy Spirit concerning the apocalyptic anointing. Despite what traditions we come from, the Holy Spirit is the giver of all these gifts. Without the Spirit's initiative, the apocalyptic anointing will not function. The source of the apocalyptic anointing is the Holy Spirit. In all these different traditions, one can learn that the Spirit works beyond denomination barriers and obstacles.

Notes

1. Erickson, Millard. *Christian Theology* (Grand Rapids: Baker Books), 1998, 863.

2. Albrecht, Daniel. *Rites in the Spirit: A Ritual Approach to Pentecostal/Charismatic Spirituality*, 218.

3. Ibid, 226-227.

4. Erickson, 876.

5. Erickson, 878.
6. Erickson, 891.
7. Pinnock, H. Clark. *Flame of Love: A Theology of the Holy Spirit* (Downers Grove: InterVarsity Press, 1996), 129.
8. Karkkainen, Veli-Matti. *Pneumatology: The Holy Spirit in Ecumenical, International, and Contextual Perspective* (Grand Rapids: Baker Academic, 2002), 15.
9. Ibid, 15.
10. Clark, 130.
11. Aker, C., Benny. *Charismata: Gifts, Enablements, or Ministries?* Journal of Pentecostal Theology. 11.1 (2002), 57.
12. Aker, 56.
13. Erickson, 891.
14. Ireland, David. *Activating the Gifts of the Holy Spirit* (New Kensington: Whitaker House, 1997), 18.
15. Ibid, 26.
16. Ibid, 27.
17. Ibid, 29.
18. Ibid, 33.
19. Ibid, 38.
20. Ibid, 39.
21. See Millard J. Erickson's *Introducing Christian Doctrine* on the theological/biblical references between trichotomy and dichotomy.
22. *The Ecumenical Review*, 305.
23. Ibid, 308.
24. Ibid, 308.
25. Warren, Rick, *The Pupose Driven Church: Growth without Compromising Your Message and Mission* (Grand Rapids: Zondervan, 1995), 371.
26. Caussade, Jean-Pierre, *The Sacrament of the Present Moment* (San Francisco: Harper, 1966), 87.
27. Nee, Watchman. *The Spiritual Man* (New York, Christian Publisher, 1977).
28. Ibid, 160.
29. Ibid, 167.
30. Ibid, 31.
31. Ibid, 32.
32. Ibid, 32.
33. Ibid, 32.
34. Ibid, 73.
35. Ibid, 77.
36. For updates in the on-going discussion of the baptism of the Holy Spirit, see Shane Clifton article: "The Spirit and Doctrinal Development: A functional Analysis of the Traditional Pentecostal Doctrine of the Baptism in the Holy Spirit," *Pneuma* 29 (2007), 5-23.

37. Macchia, Frank. *Baptized in the Spirit: A Global Pentecostal Theology.* (Grand Rapids: Zondervan, 2006), 260.
 38. Ibid, 269.
 39. Ibid, 282.

3

Various Expressions of the Apocalyptic Anointing

I never imagined I was going to be in a room with intercessors and prayer warriors in a deliverance session. We were praying for this girl who seemed to have psychological problems, but, as demons began to manifest inside her, there was no doubt in my mind she was possessed. Some people may ask how one tells the difference between demonic possession and psychological problems. When I felt the hairs on my neck standing up and saw this girl levitate in a circle up and down, I knew it was a form of possession. This girl grew up within the Santeria religion, which is a mix of pagan demonic beliefs and rituals with Roman Catholicism. As she began to call on the name of the Lord, these demons started to manifest, but Jesus, by the power of the Spirit, set her free!

The apocalyptic anointing sets people and regions free. In this chapter, we will see examples of how this anointing brings freedom. First we will consider how Paul set people and regions free in the book of Acts. We will also see examples of how deliverance and exorcism are for today. Next, we will deal with the reality that demons do not only affect humans, but they can also impact objects, places, and even creation. Therefore, we need to have a broader understanding of deliverance. Through prophetic ministry, the apocalyptic anointing speaks the will of God in bringing freedom. Finally, we receive strategies to war against the enemy to bring freedom. J. Walter Malone, a Quaker, gives us examples from his perspective of how to do spiritual warfare.

Outcomes of the Apocalyptic Anointing in Acts

The result of the apocalyptic anointing is that the light of Christ confronts the deep shadows of the underworld. For instance, on the Island of Cyprus, in a place called Paphos, the gospel of Christ confronted the power and deceit of a Jewish sorcerer named Bar-Jesus or Elymas. Elymas was an attendant to Sergius Paulus, the proconsul. A proconsul was a leader in the Roman Republic who was assigned a certain province or region to govern. The sorcerer opposed Paul, but Paul filled with the Holy Spirit and filled with discernment saw the spiritual identity of Elymas. First, Elymas is a child of the devil; second, he was an enemy of all truth; third, he was full of deceit and trickery; and fourth, he perverted the ways of the Lord. There are two main consequences in this story: first, there is an immediate punishment that comes to the sorcerer. Paul prayed that the sorcerer would lose his sight. Interestingly, Elymas was blinding people and keeping them from seeing the light of the gospel. His punishment was the same; he becomes blind. Then after the proconsul saw his attendant blind, he believed in God. The apocalyptic anointing shames and destroys the powers of the enemy in order to bring people to the saving knowledge of Jesus (Acts 13:4-12).

The apocalyptic anointing also brings deliverance when Paul confronted a slave girl who had a fortune telling spirit. As Paul and Silas were going to pray, they were confronted by the slave girl. Paul waited for the right time to cast the fortune telling spirit out. The location was Philippi. Once the owner of the slave girl realized that he could not earn more money, he stirred up trouble with the public—causing Paul and Silas to come before the magistrate to be sentenced and to be beaten. At the end of the day, they ended up in jail. In jail, both Paul and Silas began to sing praises to God—God sent an earthquake. The jailer's family got saved!

However, before they could see results of the preaching, they had to come against the spiritual and earthly opposition. The spiritual opposition was manifested through the slave girl. Then after the divination spirit was cast out (leaving a spiritual void in the life of the community), Paul and Silas dealt with humans—the slave owner, the public, and magistrate. Once that confrontation was achieved, God worked in the life of the jailer—God sends the earthquake and the jailer's family come to know Christ—this is the second outcome in this story (Acts 16:16).

The apocalyptic anointing gives us the authentic authority of Jesus' name. In Ephesus, Paul, by the power of the Spirit, performed many extraordinary miracles—this inspired seven Jewish religious men to be copycats. They tried to cast out demons in the name of Jesus. Finally, one day a demon spoke to them, and revealed their true identity. The demon or spirit acknowledged Jesus, and he knew about Paul, but who were they? This demon beats them up, teaching them a very valuable lesson to never use power without the right authority. The demon knew the power and authority of Jesus and Paul, but he also knew that these men did not have the power or the authority of Jesus (Acts 19:13).

These three incidents teach us some significant consequences of dealing with the supernatural world. First, we have power over the works of darkness—Paul had power to pray for blindness against the sorcerer. Elymas was immediately punished with his blindness. Second, Paul and Silas, after confronting the spiritual and earthly powers in Philippi, were punished by the people, but God vindicates them by releasing them from jail. Third, when one uses the wrong authority God allows us to be punished by the enemy himself, as in the case of the seven sons of Sceva.

When the apocalyptic anointing is upon a person he or she will not only see devils manifesting through people, but will have the power to cast them out, hence, the gift of exorcism. Carlos Anacondia, an Argentine evangelist who has a unique call on his life, has been a part of a revival lasting for two generations. During that time, he has witnessed many testimonies of those who were delivered from the power of darkness. In his book, *Listen to Me, Satan,* he states, "Crusade after crusade of people manifest demons. Every day, before preaching God's Word, I pray and rebuke all evil spirits that want to bring confusion and put obstacles in the minds of those who are going to hear God's Word."[1] The apocalyptic anointing gives the spiritual insight into the work of demons against people, and then it gives the power of Christ by the Spirit to cast them out.

Another result of the apocalyptic anointing is that God sets entire cities and regions free. An example of this is the seven churches in the book of Revelation; these churches were connected with the region of Asia Minor. Revelation 3:20, says, "Here I am! I stand at the door and knock. If anyone hears my voice and opens the door, I will come in and eat with him, and him with me." God in this verse was telling the Laodicean church to let him come in, but we also know that he was talking to the city of Laodicea. Churches and cities or regions are connected. When God speaks to the church, the rest of the city or region must listen to what he wants to accomplish in that community.

Deliverance Ministry

When the heavens are open, there is room for deliverance ministry, the spirit of intercession intensifies to pray for people and groups, and the anointing flows discerning with others about buildings and properties so they can be cleansed with the presence of God.

If the openness to have a deliverance ministry exists in your local church, then I suggest that a group of like-minded individuals begin to pray together and learn to minister deliverance. There are many training centers in terms of developing an inner healing and deliverance ministry. I encourage you to go about this ministry with support, proper training, education, and accountability within your local church.

Richard Ing's book *Spiritual Warfare* is also a helpful resource in how to develop a deliverance ministry. He has three chapters that overview the basics of a deliverance ministry: "Preparing Yourself to Deliver," "Preparing the Person to Be Delivered," and "Anatomy of Deliverance."

The most noteworthy advice that I have read regarding the ministry of deliverance is that, even though you are not a counselor, you need to take the time to hear people's problems before casting demons out. This includes leading people in prayer of repentance and forgiveness. If the spirit of unforgiveness is in the person, then you can shout and scream at the devil and the devils will not leave because they have a legal ground. Ing states, "Deliverance always works. If there are no manifestations for ten or fifteen minutes, that is an indication that there are areas of rights the demons are still claiming."[2]

As mentioned before, Argentina has witnessed one of the most remarkable ministries of deliverance. There, evangelist Carlos Anacondia leads crusades where he preaches the basic message of salvation and people get saved and delivered from oppression, fear, and demonic torment. His assistant in the deliverance ministry, Pablo Bottari, has overseen countless deliverance meetings and sessions for over thirty years. Bottari was just a simple barber. His religious background did not contain healings, miracles, or delivering people from satanic oppression. He was introduced to the ministry of Carlos Anacondia, and then God called him to work with the evangelist in the area of deliverance ministry.

In his book, *Free in Christ*, Pablo Bottari describes the ministry of deliverance as end time ministry that is not for elite spiritual believers, but for those who are willing to heed the call of God to set people free from bondage. He says that people need to be delivered from hatred, fear, and unbroken vows with the devil. Within the apocalyptic anointing, this ministry needs to have a place. Overall, Bottari, says, "I describe the ministry of deliverance as an End Times ministry. When the enemy is confronted with the reality of the return of Christ's coming for His Church, he tries to take advantage of every possible situation and manifests in a totally open manner."[3]

Exorcism

In the past, I had heard that the Roman Catholic Church practiced exorcism and understood that certain appointed bishops performed exorcisms. Today, however, more priests and even some lay people practice this rite. I have been intrigued to study this Catholic tradition because they have an extensive history of performing exorcism throughout centuries. Pentecostals and charismatic are still new in exercising this gift, for there are not centuries of history to rely upon. I do not agree with all Catholic exorcist methodology and teachings, such as using holy water during an exorcism. However, I feel that we can learn from these ideas. While shopping at a well-known bookstore, I came across Gabriele Amorth's second book entitled *An Exorcist: More Stories*. In June 1986, Amorth was assigned by Cardinal Ugo Poletti to go and assist Father Candido Amantini, who had 30-plus years of being an exorcist in Rome, Italy.

Amorth explains the role of an exorcist. He says, "For the most part, the exorcist's main task is to comfort the discouraged, enlighten the ignorant, and remove false fears and misguided behavior (going to magicians, card readers, and such). To do this, he must encourage souls to be reconciled with God, to resume a regular life of faith, prayers, and reception of the sacraments, as to resolve to embrace God's word."[4] This sounds similar to what the minister of deliverance tries to do within Pentecostal and charismatic circles.

Amorth relates a story of a tall, young military man who was in need of deliverance. This man only came to see him once and canceled several other appointments. Finally, he moved out of the area. Months later, Amorth received a letter telling his story of how he was prayed for and delivered from the demons that were tormenting him. A Pentecostal Evangelical group prayed for this young man. Amorth states, "I must confess that, at first, the letter was a bit disconcerting. Then I thought about the Gospel of Mark and the rebuke that John the apostle received from Jesus because of the following words: 'Teacher, we saw a man casting out demons in your name, and we forbade him, because he was not following us' (Mark 9:38). Instead, I tried to admire the faith of that community and to learn from the soldier's experience."[5] It does not matter if we are Pentecostals or Catholics; we share a common desire to see people delivered from demonic oppression and possession.

Infestations

Deliverance or exorcism can also be performed over places and objects. Amorth believes that spiritually polluted places are "infested." The church father Origen dealt with infestations. Amorth says, "From his writings, we know that exorcisms were already commonly used not only for individuals, but also for houses, objects, and animals from the early days of Christianity."[6] He continues to say, "Until the Church develops a specific language for each of these phenomena, we refer to evil disorders that affect places, objects, and animals, rather than individuals, as *Infestations*."[7] The topic of setting these things free is not easy to talk about. People do not believe until they have experienced some sort of infestation. I agree that these infestations are "so strange that they defy the imagination."[8] However, we should not fear these things.

Amorth has many examples of stories of infestations. For our purpose, I will just mention the frequent causes of infestations from his perspective. There are four causes of infestations: 1) The house was used to hold séances or magic sessions, or it was used as a base for some type of satanic cult. These infestations are the most difficult to remove. 2) Someone was killed or committed suicide in the house. 3) The house was used for prostitution or homosexual encounters or was the residence of blasphemers, Masons, criminals, leaders of criminal organizations, drug dealers, and so on. 4) The house was hexed. We need to make a full investigation of the reasons for, and methods of, the hex, because, if a cursed object is on the premises, it must be found and burned. As long as the object is in the building, no amount of prayer will bear much fruit.[9]

Now as I travel to other countries or to certain parts of a city, or to certain parts of rural areas, I can sense the demonic oppression. I am sensitive to where God is and where the demonic is operating. It is common and comes naturally for me to discern these types of activities.

My first encounter with an infested place was not a pleasant one. It was a house that we rented. There was a thick fear in the air as we went down to the basement. We called a friend of ours who was familiar with infestations. As we began to pray, our friend discerned that something terrible happened to children a long time ago in that basement.

During this experience, as we were praying, I heard a groaning so clear. I asked the Spirit, "What is that groaning?" I sensed the Spirit saying, "The earth cries every time something evil is done to God's creation." What a confirmation of Romans 8:22, where it says, "We know that the whole creation has been groaning as in the pains of childbirth right up to the present time" (NIV). But when the Spirit renews the face of the earth, creation leaps for joy in the presence of the Lord. Through our prayers and actions, the Spirit also uses us to cleanse creation from oppression and evil.

Delivering Creation

Some Christians around the world are becoming more conscious about the role of the Spirit with creation. God desires to restore his whole creation. Adam and Eve not only brought themselves under the curse of sin but also caused creation to be submitted to the power of sin and corruption. Romans 8:19-22 says, "The creation waits in eager expectation for the sons of God to be revealed. For the creation was subjected to frustration, not by its own choice, but by the will of the one who subjected it, in hope that the creation itself will be liberated from its bondage to decay and brought into the glorious freedom of the children of God. We know that the whole creation has been groaning as in the pains of childbirth right up to the present time" (NIV). The key in bringing liberation to creation is to repent and cleanse the land. It took Adam and Eve to bring curses upon the earth, and it will take the daughters and sons of God to cleanse the land with the power of the Spirit.

There is a direct connection between people and land. 2 Chronicles 7:14 , a well-known verse of the Old Testament clarifies this connection: "If my people, who are called by my name, will humble themselves and pray and seek my face and turn from their wicked ways, then I will hear from heaven and will forgive their sin and will heal their land." God promised Solomon that, if the people would repent and come to the temple, he was going to forgive their sins and heal the land. The forgiveness of sin (humans) goes hand in hand with the healing of the land (creation). You can not separate forgiveness of sins from cleansing the land from demonic infestation. The spiritual and natural environment has to be clean in order for the gospel to thrive. Often in the Old Testament, God kept his word about healing the land. The prophet Elisha heals the water in the city of Jericho. 2 Kings 2:21, says, "Then he went out to the spring and threw the salt into it, saying, "This what the Lord says: "I have healed this water. Never again will it cause death or make the land unproductive."'" As a result, the land also becomes productive. God cares for his creation.

The Spirit cares for creation. Psalms 104:30 states, "When you send your Spirit, they are created, and you renew the face of the earth." The Spirit is everywhere in creation as Psalms 139:7, says, "Where can I go from your Spirit?" Clark Pinnock explains, "The Spirit is present and active in creation—in its inception, continuation, and perfection."[10]

Ecological Dreams

This connection between the Spirit and creation is one of my favorite topics. I have done some research on Native Americans, and primarily on the Mayans of Central America concerning where they see the connection between God and the cosmos. Since I am aware of and know this topic well, of course, it is not a coincidence that God often gives me dreams of how the land has been or is being abused. One night, I had a dream in which I was in the middle of a pond. The water of the pond was filthy dirty. There were dead snakes in the pond. I found myself in the middle of the pond where the water was to my waist. Next to the pond, there was a red machine pulling coal.

At that time, I was living in an area where many coal miners came and created small towns, and then the mining companies left. They left the small towns economically in ruins. They also left the land in a desolated stage. This I saw. I saw the holes in the earth that were created by the exploiters. The Spirit allowed me to see these things in the dream so that I can pray that he will send his Spirit to renew the earth in those areas. Another example of being aware of the environment was when I went on an international mission trip to beautiful Costa Rica. There are many mountains, volcanoes, beaches, and rain forests. We stayed near the capital, which is surrounded by many mountains. Every night that we came from working on our construction project, we rested at our hotel, and, every time that I closed my eyes, I could see mountains in the spiritual realm. Then I opened my eyes, and I still could sense the mountains all around us. I did this many times; the moment I closed my eyes, I could see the mountains in the spiritual realm. I wanted to rest, not see mountains in the Spirit! The Lord taught me something important. Whatever landscape is in the natural realm, it is the same in the spiritual realm. If you are in a place where it is flat, it is flat in the spiritual realm. If there are mountains, there are mountains in the spiritual realm. This revelation blew my mind away. God cared enough to let me know that he wanted me to see what was in the spiritual realm. God does care for his creation.

Prophetic Ministry

The apocalyptic anointing can reach beyond individual deliverance and delivering places and creation, to set groups and organizations free through prophetic ministry. The prophetic is vital in speaking forth the will of God to creation. Therefore, a clear understanding of this ministry is a must!

Much has been written in recent years about the ministry of the prophetic, encouraging the pastor or leader to embrace the prophetic. In order to embrace the prophetic, one needs to understand the sole purpose of the prophetic ministry. Eileen Fisher, in her book, *Embracing the Prophetic*, states that the prophetic work is "to build, edify, encourage, and strengthen the Body of Christ."[11] The prophetic people have to embrace and understand proper authority in order to work as a team in the church. Fisher lays the biblical foundation from both Old Testament and New Testament scriptures that speak about the prophetic ministry.

The essential keys to having a prophetic ministry in the local church are proper communication and proper understanding of the prophetic gift. The ministry of the prophetic can assimilate easily into a church if the pastor or leadership has some sort of understating of the prophetic gift. Mike Bickle, in his book *Growing in the Prophetic*, includes a chapter entitled, "Pastors and Prophets: Getting Along in the Kingdom." Bickle concludes that pastors and prophets must work together: "Unless we learn to show honor to each other and to the unique work that the Holy Spirit is doing in each person's life, we may wind up in a holy war, especially if the gifts and personalities are strong. Without team ministry, none of these gifts would be able to prosper. I believe this is especially true for the prophetic ministry."[12]

Testing of the Prophetic

R. Loren Sandford, in his book *Understanding Prophetic People: Blessings and Problems with the Prophetic Gift*, outlines several blessings and issues with prophetic people and with prophetic words. He freely acknowledges that prophetic people often have eccentric personalities, are self-protected because of rejection, deal with loneliness and isolation, and seem extreme and moody.

Sandford explains his negative experiences in having an open mic to give prophecy in his church. He writes, "quite honestly, 99 percent of what came forth was vapid sentimentality that merely took up air space, inflated the speaker's own sense of importance and edified no one...the other 1 percent was mostly harmful condemnation by people looking for a platform from which to vent the spleen of their personal judgments."[13] As a result of these negative experience, he decided to cultivate a group of mature people who operated in the prophetic. Sanford developed in his church a small group that tests the validity and character of the prophetic people. First, this small group is grounded in the Bible—they read and study the word of God to bring balance to their gifting. Second, within this group leaders and pastors are able to tell how "prophetic people quickly emerge and we learn who is reliable, humble and broken...on the other hand, immature people, or those with unresolved issues of rejection,...the test then becomes one of correctability and humility."[14] This stage is important because this will decide who stays in this small group, who rises up to the challenge to continue to grow in their gifts. Third, this group writes down 'God dreams' or prophetic insight for the church, and then submit them to the pastor. This is another way to stay accountable to the leadership of the church. There is a danger to this way of testing; it can lead to control and manipulation if not done properly on the part of the leadership team. Sanford states, "Fourth, our church places a high value on ministry teams composed of trained and sensitive laypeople."[15] This is where they pray for healing, life situations, spiritual breakthrough, and anything else that needs prayer. In this small group, they only allow a few people who are accountable to each other and to the leadership of the church. This kind of group is needed in churches where the prophetic is emphasized, but all leaders and workers must have proper accountability to benefit and strength the body of Christ.

The prophetic gift, which often manifests itself in dreams and visions, is essential for the apocalyptic anointing, that seeks to set individuals, groups, and locations free from the hold of demons and Satan's control. The Spirit is working to restore God's creation into the perfect unity and form in which it was created. The Spirit uses human beings through spiritual gifts to bring about the restoration of the world back to God. When one steps into these things, he or she engages in spiritual warfare.

Warfare

Finally, it is vital to draw from different streams of spiritual traditions in order to hear a cohesive voice concerning how the Holy Spirit works in the supernatural through spiritual gifts. Much of what we hear about the supernatural within Christian circles comes primarily from the Pentecostal/charismatic circles; thus, some are hesitant to study the topic or trust the literature from these groups. In an effort to move us away from this stereotype, this section will bring a voice from outside the Pentecostal/charismatic circles—that of J. Walter Malone, a Quaker.

J. Walter Malone

Even before the birth of the modern day Pentecostal movement at the Azusa Street Revival in 1905, the Holiness movement, within the Wesleyan tradition, was holding revival services. The services led by John Wesley and others influenced other Christian traditions. One of these traditions was the Quakers. They also had their own revivals and spiritual experiences.

John W. Oliver, in his book *J. Walter Malone: the Autobiography of an Evangelical Quaker*, describes the life of Malone.[16] J. Walter Malone was born August 11, 1857, on a farm in Clermont County, Ohio, not far from Cincinnati. His parents were pious and godly Quakers. In order to understand Malone's spiritual background, one has to consider carefully the life of his mother. Malone said, "Mother was a very loving, saved, and Spirit-filled Woman, aggressive in religious matters, and wanting everyone to have the same experience that she had."[17] As Walter describes the spiritual experiences of his mother Mary Anne, it is evident that he was intrigued to see that she had a prophetic spirit. One day when she was interceding for God to give her a house, she heard God telling her to get up from her knees because he was going to send the answer to her prayers. God sent a business person to help her buy a house for a low price.[18]

Walter Malone personally witnessed the spiritual realm after the first Quaker revival that ran five weeks. During that time in February 1881, 150 persons professed conversion or were renewed. Around that time, Mary Anne gave a prophetic word. Walter described it as "an inspiration and a prophetic vision in which she saw a great outpouring of the Holy Spirit bringing a gracious revival."[19] One can only wonder if she was talking about the great Azusa Street Revival that happened in California around 1905.

Walter's own spiritual experience included the baptism of the Holy Spirit. He described his baptism in the Holy Spirit: "Suddenly and blessedly...I felt myself in the atmosphere of love, Divine love of melting tenderness, not known heretofore; a love for everyone and a longing for every minister and every Christian to receive this fullness of the blessing of the Gospel."[20] It is intriguing to see that he describes the baptism of the Holy Spirit as a baptism of love and not of tongues.

Spiritual Warfare and Visions: A Quaker Perspective

After having this baptism, J. Walter Malone's eyes were opened to the spiritual realm. God showed him a vision of a terrible dragon that was after him. Malone explained, "And just in front of me was the terrible dragon with a terrible mouth open, showing terrible teeth. It had terrible feet with powerful wings, which had on them long sharp claws that he raised to strike me down. Yet each time that he raised his black pinions to strike me, I would say, 'Jesus, Jesus' and take a step forward, and his dragon wings would fall short of me."[21] This vision gave Walter the assurance that through the name of Jesus he was more than a conqueror, that he had power over his enemy.

Demons of sickness began to manifest in his ministry—"Another time when we were praying for the sick, my wife and I were to lay our hands on this afflicted one, rebuke demons, and bid them to come out. The Lord opened my eyes to see the demons, and the impression is with me still as clearly as it was on that day. I can still see the angry creature showing his teeth and fiery eyes and growling at us."[22]

The most impressive step of obedience for J. Walter Malone was the Spirit leading him to open a Bible college to train young people in the ministry of evangelism and missions. There was a struggle, but eventually he opened what is now known as Malone College in Canton, Ohio. To me, his life is quite impressive; he not only relied on the subjective work of the Spirit, but he founded a Bible institute out of a desire to balance it by training people intellectually as well as spiritually.

We have noted how the apocalyptic anointing expresses itself in the life of the believer. The Spirit uses the believer to bring restoration to his creation. Next we will look at how God reveals to us his view through dreams and visions.

Notes

1. Anacondia, Carlos, *Listen To Me, Satan* (Lake Mary: Creation House, 1998), 65.

2. Ing, Richard, *Spiritual Warfare* (New Kensington: Whitaker House, 1996), 201.

3. Bottari, Pablo, *Free in Christ: Your Complete Handbook on the Ministry of Deliverance* (Lake Mary: Charisma House, 2000), 47.

4. Amorth, Gabriele, *An Exorcist: More Stories* (San Francisco: Ignatius Press, 2002) 11.

5. Ibid, 125.

6. Ibid, 155.

7. Ibid, 155.

8. Ibid, 155.

9. Ibid, 158.

10. Pinnock, 53.

11. Fisher, Eileen, *Embracing the Prophetic: A Handbook for Seeing and Hearing the Supernatural.* (Shippensburg: Destiny Image, 2007), 11.

12. Bickle, Mike, *Growing in the Prophetic.* (Lake Mary: Creation House, 1996), 146.

13. Sandford, Loren, R., *Understanding Prophetic People: Blessings and Problems with the Prophetic Gift* (Grand Rapids: Chosen Books, 2007), 223.

14. Ibid, 224-225.

15. Ibid, 225.

16. Oliver, John. *J. Walter Malone: The Autobiography of an Evangelical Quaker* (Lanham: University Press of America, 1993).

17. Ibid, 1.

18. Ibid, 2-6.

19. Ibid, 8.

20. Ibid, 49—footnote F.

21. Ibid, 56.

22 Ibid, 57.

4

Interpreting Apocalyptic Dreams and Visions

The apocalyptic anointing reveals the supernatural through dreams and visions. It is important to understand the different types of dreams and visions because, the more we are aware of them, the better we are able to see what God and what the enemy are doing in the spiritual realm. This chapter will explore the expression of the apocalyptic anointing through dreams and visions. The narrative method of interpretation will be applied to the book of Revelation. This approach is helpful in making sense of apocalyptic dreams and visions. After understanding the content of dreams and visions, one must respond to what God is saying.

Biblical Foundation

Dreams and visions are avenues by which God speaks to his people as well as to those who do not know him. God spoke in dreams and visions in the Old Testament and New Testament. Two scripture references in the Old Testament are commonly mentioned in books that talk about dreams. The first reference is Job 33:14-16, "In a dream, in a vision of the night, when deep sleep falls on men as they slumber in their beds, he may speak in their ears and terrify them with warnings, to turn man from wrongdoing and keep him from pride, to preserve his soul from the pit, his life from perishing by the sword" (NIV). Paying attention to our dreams may save our lives one day.

The Second reference is Number 12:6-8, "Listen to my words: "When a prophet of the LORD is among you, I reveal myself to him in visions, I speak to him in dreams. However, this is not true of my servant Moses; he is faithful in my entire house. With him, I speak face to face, clearly and not in riddles; he sees the form of the LORD. Why then were you not afraid to speak against my servant Moses?" Moses had an intimate relationship with God and was allowed to talk with God face-to-face. The apocalyptic anointing could lead us beyond dreams and visions into an encounter with the risen Christ.

Understanding the Dreams You Dream, by Ira Milligan, describes the process of interpretation of dreams and visions. The first thing to understand is what type of dream you are seeing. Milligan says about dreams, "A dream is like a snapshot, which captures one brief moment out of life. It cannot be understood fully without knowing something about the life of the person it concerns."[1] He goes on to differentiate, "A night vision requires little or no interpretation. In addition to the actual vision seen, a night vision usually has a voice speaking that gives the primary meaning and message of the vision"[2] When one receives a vision while asleep, the vision is more vivid than a dream and more direct in its message.

Dreams are more obscure. One of the ways to interpret a dream accurately is by paying attention to the first scene of the dream. Ira believes that the first scene of the dream introduces the subject. An example of this is the dream progression of Daniel 4:20-27. Daniel interpreted Nebuchadnezzar's dream by beginning with the first scene that established the success of the king. He saw a strong and high tree that grew fruitful and covered the earth. He moved to the second scene and interpreted it in light of the first. A watcher declared that the tree would be cut down and stumped, banded with iron and brass. The king's success stood in stark contrast to the judgment that would come because of his disobedience. God gave Daniel the ability to interpret the subtle details of the dream. Paying attention to a dream's sequence of scene, and notable detail are keys to dream interpretation.

The right application of the dream can be determined by answering the following questions—to whom does this dream refer, and what are the people saying and doing? Normally dreams are about the dreamer, the person who is dreaming the dream. Another important factor in interpreting the dream is to maintain the awareness of where the dream originates. There are three main sources of dreams: God, Satan, and the human spirit.

Emotions are important in interpreting dreams. The emotions after we wake up can be misleading, but the emotions while we are having the dream seem to be accurate in most cases. Colors are also important in dreams, so we have to pay attention to them. The most difficult question for interpretation is determining if the dreams are literal or symbolic. Ira says, "As a general rule, if a dream can be taken literally, it should be. If there is something in a dream that is not literal, however, then the entire dream should be interpreted as if the objects, and sometimes even the people it contains, are symbols."[3] This question is not only a problem in dreams but as I will later point out, it becomes a greater dilemma in apocalyptic literature.

Some dreams are warnings; this means that the outcome of the dream can change. The classic example of this is found in Amos 7:1-6. When God shows the prophet the judgments that he is going to bring upon his people and the prophet prays for God not to do that, God hears and does not bring the judgments. Finally, remember that if the same dream is repeated several times, then God is trying to convey the message in dreams in a very accurate way.

A comprehensive work on dreams is the book by James W. and Michal Ann Goll entitled, *Dream Language: the prophetic power of dreams, revelations, and the spirit of wisdom*. According to this book, spiritual dreams are a gift God gives to communicate his will to his children. Goll outlines three categories of dreams: 1) God speaking to our spirit; 2) Our spirit crying out to God; 3) God's Spirit interceding through our spirit. Goll states, "I love it when He awakens me in the night and my spirit cries out to him. And I love it when His Spirit, in union with mine, intercedes and even enters a spiritual warfare arena through a dream or other God Encounters."[4] Dreams and visions with the apocalyptic anointing can take the dreamer into warfare. Warfare depends upon the leading of God—it is not just about rebuking demons, but discerning the strategies of the enemy and then allowing God to enter into battle. After all, it is His battle not ours.

Critical Narrative Approach

There is a general process of interpreting the Bible, but the symbolic nature of apocalyptic literature presents a number of difficulties. One of the challenges is understanding the continuity of prophecy from the Old Testament to the New Testament. The Old Testament prophets can shed light into the way prophecy is used in the New Testament. Christopher R. Seitz, in his textbook, *Prophecy and Hermeneutics*, writes that the minor prophet Jonah introduces the concept that the ultimate purpose of God is that all people need to be saved, not only the Jews. Seitz, states, "This new form, which might be called apostolic prophecy, has implications that we have not yet worked out or perhaps even fully grasped." He further says, "Apostolic prophecy will pick up the old prophetic torch before it sits too long on the damp ground of its own dissolution."[5] Just as apostolic prophesy is a new issue in biblical interpretation (hermeneutics), apocalyptic revelations cause us to wrestle with the obscurities of its content and biblical symbolism.

One possible solution is moving from "hermeneutics of suspicion" to "hermeneutics of welcome." Hermeneutics of suspicion is an "objective model," which stressed a scientific distinction between "what the text said" and "how it is applied." In other words, it is a closed, rigid system. Opposite to this view, is the hermeneutics of welcome, which according to Edith M. Humphrey is, "by in large, on the 'openness' of the text and the multivalent potential that it provides for the imaginative and/or caused engaged reader." This happens when one moves from merely being logical (Verbal, Polemic, Closed: appealing to logic) to being more imaginative (Visual, Symbolic, Open: appealing to the imagination).[6] This imaginative way is achieved by rhetorical analysis.[7] Next is an introduction to apocalyptic literature of interpretation.

Apocalyptic Hermeneutics

Henry Virkler and Karelynne Gerber Ayayo, in their second edition of *Hermeneutics: Principles and Processes of Biblical Interpretation*, bring a distinction between prophetic and apocalyptic literature and point out some similarities that co-exist between these special literary forms. For our purpose, we are concentrating on what constitutes apocalyptic literature. "Apocalyptic literature's primary focus is the revelation of what has been hidden, particularly with regard to the end times."[8] There are nine features of this literature. The first feature is the writer chooses a great man of the past, such as Enoch or Moses, and makes him a hero of the book. A second feature is that whatever hero the writer chooses takes a journey, accompanied by a celestial guide who shows him interesting sights and comments on them. Third, information is often communicated through visions, Fourth, the visions frequently make use of strange, even enigmatic symbolism. Fifth, the visions are pessimistic with the possibilities that human intervention will improve the present situation. Sixth, the vision usually ends with God destroying things and establishing better ones. Seventh, the writer uses a false name, the name of his chosen hero. Eighth, the writer takes past history and rewrites it as if it were prophecy. Finally, nine, the focus of apocalyptic literature is on comforting and sustaining the "righteousness remnant."[9]

George Ladd identifies three features of apocalyptic writings. The first is the emergence of a "Righteous Remnant." Usually, this is a minority group who does not have political power and who views itself as faithful to God. A second feature is the "problem of evil." The third feature is that "apocalyptists attempted to bring a word of comfort and reassurance from God to the people of their day."[10] Of the three features, confronting the problem of evil is key to the apocalyptic anointing.

In his article, Professor L. Michael White emphasizes the problem of evil as a cosmic battle. White states, "Most *apocalyptic literature* tends to portray the history of the world as a cosmic conflict between God and some evil force, usually called Satan. It's important to note, therefore, that the extremely influential legend of how Satan was an angel in Heaven who rebelled against God and was cast out only arises with the writing of *1 Enoch*, in ca. 225 BCE. This work of Jewish apocalyptic transforms older Near Eastern combat myths into the scheme for this dualistic battle between God (good) and Satan (evil)."[11] Apocalyptic dreams and visions are about this fight against evil that goes on hidden from the natural eye. God and his angels are actively fighting to establish his kingship here on earth.

There are many schools of thought regarding the interpretation of the book of Revelation. The critical narrative method is one way of understanding this complex book. Even though one may not be familiar with the narrative approach of interpretation, it is vital to understand it. When the revelations of God come to those carrying this apocalyptic anointing, this method will help to understand what God is saying through dreams and visions.

Narrative Critical Method—Jim Ressegguie

There is much written on interpreting the book of Revelation from a narrative perspective. I am going to summarize the basics for interpreting the book of Revelation from a narrative point of view. In his book, *Revelation Unsealed: A Narrative Critical Approach to John's Apocalypse*, J. L. Resseguie states, "The purpose is to enter John's narrative world, to see what he sees, and to stand where he stands."[12] In other words, nothing external can be brought into the visions that John saw, but the interpretation itself pays attention to the characters, props, worlds, etc...From there one is able to interpret the book of Revelation.

The narrative method focuses on setting (the physical and sometimes spiritual background against which the action of a narrative takes place), rhetoric (how the story is told to create certain effects on the readers), point of view (first person narration: I, or third person narration: he, she, and they), characters (the persons, animals, angelic, and demonic beings presented in a vision or dream), and plot (the order in which the story is told; its events and actions).[13]

Point of View

The point of view seeks to find from the different sources what the story or narrative tells us. It analyzes the story's beliefs and values, as well as the message it is trying to persuade us to believe (ideological or theological). The point of view also finds thoughts, expressions, and feelings and evaluates what is going on from a (psychological) perspective. The point of view pays close attention to language and grammar that the story is using (phraseological). Timing is essential to point of view. It tries to find the past, present, and future tense of the narrative (temporal). Finally, point of view centers on whether the narrative is talking about its characters or locations, whether they are public or private—it also deals with the arrangement of props: landscape, trees, and birds, wind etc. Refer to figure 1 to see how all these are connected and related to each other.[14]

Point of View Book of Revelation

There are several examples that will be given from the book of

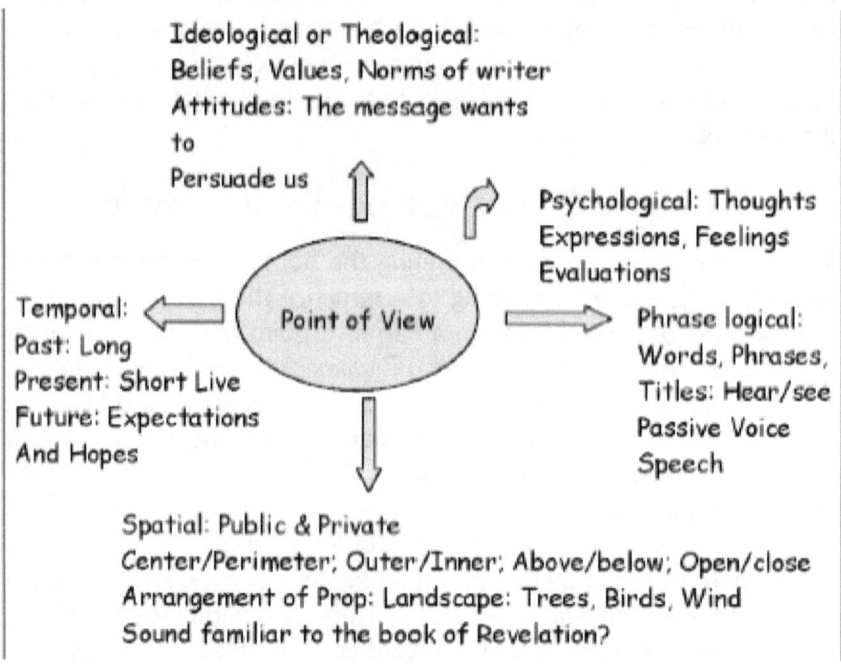

Figure 1

The point of view includes the phraseological, spatial, psychological, temporal and ideological, when the actions, setting, and events are mediated through the narrator's perspective.[15]

Revelation in terms of the point of view. For a complete understanding in this approach, see Jim Resseguie's book.

The simplest thing to add here is to say that even though there are some big words in this narrative process—the key is to pay careful attention to all the details that are in the dream or vision. The narrative approach puts them in categories so it can make it easy for us to understand what the vision means. Let us look at the example of point of view from the ideological or theological perspective.

This is an example of the ideological point of view, or the message that is trying to persuade us. Revelation, 1:12-20, says,

I turned around to see the voice that was speaking to me. And when I turned I saw seven golden lampstands,

and among the lampstands was someone "like a son of man," dressed in a robe reaching down to his feet and with a golden sash around his chest.

His head and hair were white like wool, as white as snow, and his eyes were like blazing fire.

His feet were like bronze glowing in a furnace, and his voice was like the sound of rushing waters.

In his right hand he held seven stars, and out of his mouth came a sharp double-edged sword. His face was like the sun shining in all its brilliance.

When I saw him, I fell at his feet as though dead. Then he placed his right hand on me and said: "Do not be afraid. I am the First and the Last.

I am the Living One; I was dead, and behold I am alive for ever and ever! And I hold the keys of death and Hades.

"Write, therefore, what you have seen, what is now and what will take place later.

The mystery of the seven stars that you saw in my right hand and of the seven golden lampstands is this: The seven stars are the angels of the seven churches, and the seven lampstands are the seven churches (NIV).

The character in this chapter is Jesus. Jesus in this vision is burnished by the fire, which represents the purity of Christ. His feet were glowing like the bronze in the furnace, which represents the image of stability. The conclusion comes after examining that bronze is heavy, is metal, is an alloy, which represents something that is not going to break easy. Jesus' head and hair were like wool, which represent the righteousness. His eyes were like a flame of fire, this means that he can penetrate and sees beneath the surface of the false appearances—he sees the reality of things as they are. Jesus had seven stars in his right hand, the right hand represents his sovereignty and authority upon the churches. Therefore, the message of Christ in this vision is that Christ is pure, righteous, stable, and he can see what is false because of his sovereignty and authority. Christ is able to see the spiritual conditions of the seven churches—their purity as well as their shortcomings and faults.

In visions and dreams, it is important to see and to hear what message is being conveyed. John, in his visions, mixes events he sees with what is heard; what he hears interprets what he sees. For instance, at the conclusion of each letter to the churches, there is a saying, "He who has an ear, let him hear what the Spirit is saying to the churches" (2:7, 11, 17, 29; 3:6, 13, 22). In the same way, after the beast rises out of the sea, John records a command to hear (13:9-10). The hearing places the seeing in a new perspective.[16]

Characters

Moving from point of view, let us consider the character. In a story or narrative, paying attention to characters takes note of what they are doing, wearing, thinking, saying, and who is speaking to the character. Figure 2 [See next page] demonstrates how the character is connected to his actions, motives, beliefs, sayings, and so on and so forth.

After identifying who the characters are: God, man, woman, animals both—God's or Satan's, beasts etc...; we then pay attention to what the character is doing, saying, thinking and what the writer is saying about the character. Some characters from the book of Revelation are animals. There are two types of animals in Revelation: 1) demonic animals—locusts, birds, the dragon and beasts—creatures of the world below; and 2) Apocalyptic animals—the four living creatures, Lamb and eagle—animals from the world above.[17] All these characters dwell and fight each other in three realms. John operates in three realms in these apocalyptic visions. See Figure 3 to see John's world in Revelations.[18]

The following chapters in the book of Revelation will explain how this world operates and interacts. In chapter four of Revelation, there are four living creatures, which are apocalyptic animals or beings. These apocalyptic animals are from the world above, where there are open

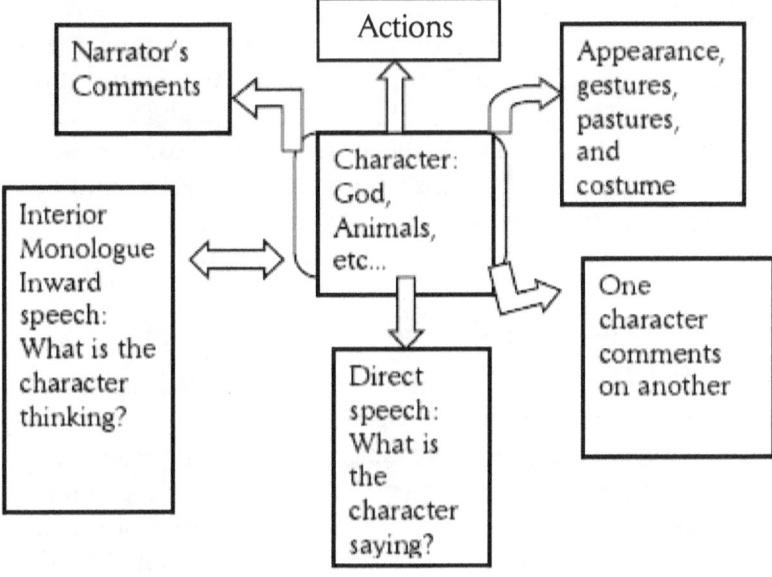

Figure 2

heavens to see the throne. There are two witnesses who came down from heaven, and they go back to heaven after the sea beast defeats them (Rev. 11). Revelation 12 talks about the war in the heavens of Michael and the dragon, and the dragon was thrown to earth (where

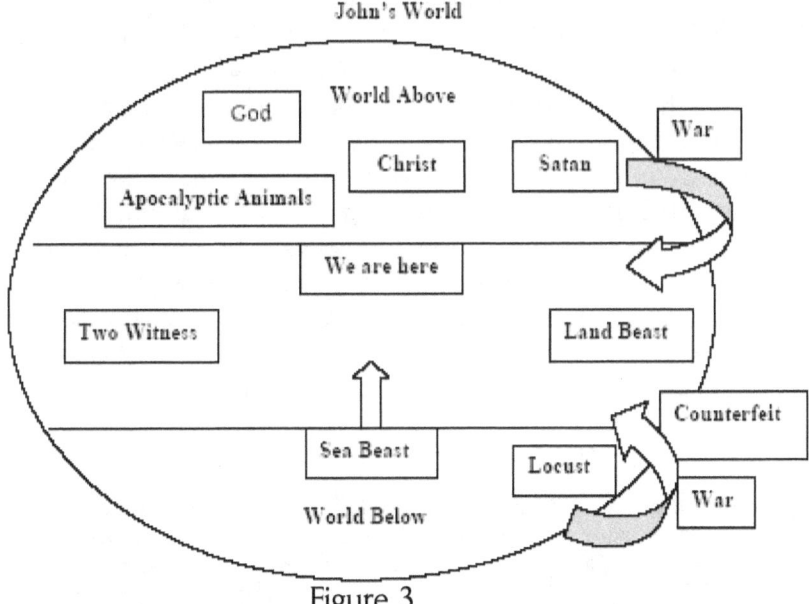

Figure 3

humans dwell).

In Revelation 9:3, there are locusts, which come from the world below, the bottomless pit. In Revelation 13, the land beast and the sea beast come from the pit to cause chaos upon the land. The person who has the apocalyptic anointing is able to relate to the world of John—the world above, the world below, and where everything comes head to head here on earth. When a person operates in the apocalyptic anointing he or she will become familiar with these worlds.

Applying the Narrative Approach

The following is an example of how to apply the narrative method, particularly the spatial point of view: center and perimeter. Jim Resseguie says, "John focuses on an object at the center of his visions and then pans outward to describe the perimeter, or he describes the perimeter and then narrows to focus on the center. Since the center of his vision is what he wants the reader to focus on, it represents not only what is most important in his visions but also the core of his theology."[19] First, the vision of the throne in Revelation chapter four focuses on the character who is sitting on the throne, then it moves to the perimeter where he sees other characters and props such as the four living creatures, the seven flaming torches, and something like a sea of crystal.

Other Hebrew prophets had seen the same visions with different details. The prophet Daniel in chapter seven of his book describes a similar vision. Daniel 7:9-10 states, "Thrones were set in place and an Ancient One took his throne, his clothing was white as snow, and the hair of his head like pure wool; his throne was fiery flames, and its wheels burning fire. A stream of fire issued and flowed out from his presence..." (NRSV). The focus is on the Ancient One or the Ancient of Days, and then it moves to the flaming river that is around his throne. These two visions share common point of view, but, by focusing on the character's actions, narrator's comments, and props, we are left with a very different understanding of each. John brings us to awe and deep worship, while Daniel recognizes the rule and dominion of God.

It is astounding to find an account of a similar vision in the Jewish apocalyptic literature.

1 Enoch 71:5-12 says:

> He carried off my spirit, and I, Enoch, was in the heaven of heavens. There I saw—in the midst of that light—a structure built of crystals; and between those crystals tongues of living fire. And my spirit saw a ring, which encircled this structure of fire. On its four sides were rivers full of living fire, which encircled.

> Moreover, seraphim, cherubim, and ophanim—the sleepless ones who guard the throne of his glory—also encircled it...with them is the Antecedent of Time: His head is white and pure like wool and his garment is indescribable.[20]

Enoch primarily focuses on the outside perimeter of the throne, and then describes the one who is sitting on the throne. It is fascinating to notice that between those crystal structures were *tongues of living fire*. Both John and Daniel see fire around the throne but Enoch sees the fire as *tongues of living fire*. Again the narrative approach allows us to consider each detail and fully understand the significant differences of each revelation. My Pentecostal upbringing reminds me of the other reference that we see to tongues of fire in the book of Acts.

When the Spirit was poured out in the book of Acts, there were tongues of fire on the disciples. Acts 2:3-4, says, "Divided tongues, as of fire, appeared among them, and a tongue rested on each of them. All of them were filled with the Holy Spirit and began to speak in other languages, as the Spirit gave them ability" (NRSV). One cannot deny that there are tongues of fire that rested on the disciples as a sign of his presence and as a sign to those who do not believe in him, because the people understood what the disciples were saying in their native tongue. The emphasis is not on the tongues of fire, but on the one who is sitting on the throne. The tongues of fire should lead people to see the one who is sitting on the throne.

Paul tells us in 1 Corinthians 13:12, "Now we see through a glass darkly." God may reveal the same vision or dream to different people, but the emphasis and meaning may change as God speaks directly to individuals, groups, or regions.

Contemporary Visions of Satanic Networks

Examples of modern day visions are those received by Mary Baxter. She has seen some intense apocalyptic visions of hell and heaven. One of the revelations that God gave her is about the horns that the prophet Daniel spoke of. First, consider Daniel's vision. He sees four beasts rising out of the roaring sea. The fourth beast troubles Daniel the most. Daniel inquires about the fourth beast. Daniel 7:20 says, "and concerning the ten horns that were on its head, and concerning the other horn, which came up to make room for which three of them fell out—the horn that had eyes and a mouth that spoke arrogantly..." (NRSV). The interpretation that is given to Daniel is that this horn is a kingdom on earth that was going to be different from other evil kingdoms in the world. Evil reproduces itself; in the vision in Daniel, from one horn other horns come out from the pits.

God showed Mary Baxter a similar vision. She saw the heart of hell and out of the heart came arteries, arms or horns. She says, "Coming out from this black heart were what looked like large arms or horns. They were coming out of it and going up and out of hell into the earth."[21] It is best to let Mary expound on these horns. She writes:

> Jesus said, "These branches, which look like arteries of a heart, are pipelines that go up through the earth to spill evil upon it. These are the horns that Daniel saw, and they represent evil kingdoms on the earth...out of these main branches or horns, smaller branches will grow. Out of the smaller branches will come demons, evil spirits and all manner of evil forces. They will be released upon the earth and instructed by Satan to do many evil works...Dark clouds came out of the horns and hid many forms of evil that were going out upon the earth...I saw the old horns removed and new ones grow in their places.[22]

Both Daniel and Mary Baxter received apocalyptic visions that reveal the end time workings of demonic spirits related to regions and nations. As we understand our enemy we can better pray and wage war to advance the kingdom of God.

One night, I had a dream of a strong man, riding this black horse was a strong man and on top of the strong man was a principality. This dream revealed to me how different spiritual networks operate and how they are organized. In the dream, I was in the woods, and then I came to a military camp where there was a train station. I moved to a door where it was all dark. It was in this dark place that the principality was dwelling—I saw in this camp young men getting in shape for battle. Then I went through a tunnel and out of the camp. The principality did not see me because his camp was hit on the other side with flashing lighting. I knew it was looking for me, but it never found me. In this dream, I was able to understand that the enemy has tunnels and underground networks beneath the earth that are interconnected from one region to another region and from one country to others. This is no joke! This stuff is real.

These underground tunnels are part of hell as Mary Baxter describes. The enemy has an underground network that moves in planning and plotting his destructive and evil acts upon the earth and upon humanity. For the first time in my life, I was able to see these tunnels or portals with my spiritual eyes and ask the Lord to close and destroy them. By destroying these underground tunnels, one gains territorial ground that the enemy had used to funnel evil spirits like serpents and scorpions. Since then, I have seen portals and tunnels in other places. This is regional spiritual warfare.

Had I not paid attention to this dream, I would have never gained the territory that God wanted to set free or engage in warfare. When you see the work of the enemy in the spiritual realm it is for a purpose. God wants to stop the flow of evil that is spewed upon the earth. These gates and passageways destroy the lives of individuals and the work of the church. You must be aware of your dreams and discern what God is revealing through scripture and ongoing revelations to other Christians. Moving from the intense visions of the book of Revelation, we come to how we respond to dreams and visions. The critical narrative method helps us to interpret them; this next section will teach us to respond appropriately.

Correct Response to Dreams and Visions

Herman Riffel's *Dream Interpretation* emphasizes the importance of paying attention to the dreams that we dream. Riffel says, "We will not remember our dreams for long if we do not respond to them. That principle applies to the teachings of the Scriptures as well. If we disregard what we hear from God, we will soon lose our understanding of what He is saying."[23] To illustrate this point, Riffel gives the biblical example of Jacob: "Jacob's dream of the ladder up to heaven with the angels of God ascending and descending on it told him that the way of access to heaven was open for him... God waited twenty years for Jacob to respond properly to the dream He had given him."[24] The one who has the apocalyptic anointing has to be careful to respond correctly to the dreams and revelations of God in order to fulfill his will here on earth.

Most of the time, dreams and visions are warnings. It is important to journal our dreams and visions so we can remember what God has spoken to us. At times, dreams may not make sense to us immediately, but as we look back on them, we may see a series of related dreams or understand what God was revealing to us for an appointed time. Many do not know what to do with their dreams and visions—they get overwhelmed or simply disregard them. One of the ways not to get overwhelmed is to recount the dream or vision, and then pray it back to

God. In other words, pray for the interpretation, but even if God does not provide the interpretation, one has to still pray through the dream. You say, "Lord, you showed me this dream, and this is what the dream is. Lord, there must be a reason why you showed me this dream—let your will be done in this dream or vision." In these last days, we must pay attention and interpret the Spirit's revelations.

Notes

1. Milligan, Ira. *Understanding the Dreams You Dream* (Shippensburg: Destiny Image, 1997), 6.
2. Ibid, 7-8.
3. Ibid, 23.
4. Goll, James and Ann. *Dream Language: The Prophetic Power of Dreams, Revelations, and the Spirit of Wisdom* (Shippensburg: Destiny Image, 2006), 45.
5. Seitz, Christopher. *Prophecy and Hermeneutics: Toward a New Introduction to the Prophets.* (Grand Rapids: Baker Academic, 2007), 23.
6. Edith Humbrey. *And I Turned to See the Voice: The Rhetoric of Vision in the New Testament* (Grand Rapids: Baker Academics, 2007), , 28.
7. This is Edith Humfrey's approach to the rhetoric of vision in the New Testament. She defines rhetorical analysis as "interested in the speech craft of the writer (sometimes as put into the mouth or a character in the text), in the persuasive power of the speech itself (as encoded in the text), and in the effect on the listener (i.e., characters listening within the text, the implied reader, the reader more-or-less contemporary with the writer, and other subsequent readers)," 23.
8. Virkler, Henry, and Ayayo, Karelynne. *Hermeneutics: Principles and Processes of Biblical Interpretation* (Grand Rapids: Baker Academics, 2007), 176.
9. Ibid, This is Leon Morris categorization (I paraphrase some of them), 176.
10. Ibid, 176.
11. White, Michael. *The Antichrist: A Historical Puzzle.* http://www.pbs.org/wgbh/pages/frontline/shows/apocalypse/antichrist/white.html.
12. Resseguie, J. L. *Revelation Unsealed: A Narrative Critical Approach to John's Apocalypse* (Leiden: Brill, 1998).
13. Ibid., 1.
14. NT 629 Book of Revelation—class notes. Fall 2003, Winebrenner Theological Seminary—Professor, James L. Resseguie.
15. Ibid., 32. Figure 1 came out of the class notes that I took on this book.
16. Ibid, 33.
17. Ibid., 103.
18. NT 629 Book of Revelation—class notes. Fall 2003, Winebrenner Theological Seminary—Professor, James L. Resseguie.

19. Ibid, 38.

20. Charlesworth, James. Volume 1. *The Old Testament Pseudepigrapha: Apocalyptic Literature and Testaments* (New York: Doubleday, 1983).

21. Baxter, Mary. *The Divine Revelation of Hell* (Sprindale: Whitaker House, 1993), 104.

22. Ibid, 105 and 123.

23. Riffel, Herman. *Dream Interpretation: A Biblical Understanding.* (Shippensburg: Destiny Image, 1993), 35.

24. Ibid, 37.

5

Apocalyptic Symbolism and Warfare

During a season of warfare, I and another brother were praying in a church. God began to reveal to us the demonic oppression that was throughout the building and property. Starting in the sanctuary and moving to each room, God opened our spiritual eyes. Through the spirit, we saw many different animals on the walls, ceiling, and floor. We spent a better part of the afternoon in prayer and warfare to cleanse this church building from these demonic influences. In each room, we saw a different evil manifestation and prayed specifically as the Holy Spirit directed us. Immediately, God responded to our prayers, and our eyes were opened to see his strategies attack and destroy the demonic critters.

We were not seeking this type of experience and had not even planned to pray that day, but God began to give us insight. At first, I was surprised, but there was a sweet and powerful anointing that drove away our fear and doubt and enabled us to obey God's direction. As we witnessed the spiritual realities our faith grew. Our prayers took on a new authority given by the Spirit.

As you walk in the apocalyptic anointing you will encounter the enemy. Third level warfare reveals the demonic strategies over a region, and often those strategies include demonic animals. The narrative method equips us to understand these demonic characters. God also has ranks of angels and apocalyptic animals that engage and combat the demonic forces. Both demonic and apocalyptic animals can be found in the book of Revelation, throughout scripture, and in intertestamental literature such as in the book of Enoch.

Demonic Animals

Demonic animals in Revelation include locusts, frogs, birds in midheaven, dragons/serpents, and beasts (sea and land). The reference to birds in mid-heaven is Revelation 19:17-18, 21. These demonic birds gather in a funeral banquet to eat the flesh of the dead and kings in the "great supper of God" (19:17). Another scripture reference is Revelation 18:2 which states, "...fallen! Fallen is Babylon the Great! She has become a home for demons and a haunt for every unclean spirit, a haunt for every unclean and detestable bird" (NIV). There is a close association between demons and unclean spirits with unclean birds. John Eckhardt, in his book *Prayers That Rout Demons,* says about demons and animals, "Demons are also represented by different creatures. The Bible talks about serpents, scorpions, jackals, bulls, foxes, owls, sea serpents, flies, and dogs. These represent different kinds of evil spirits that operate to destroy human kind. They are invisible to the natural eye. They are just as real, however, as natural creatures."[1]

Snakes, Serpents, and Scorpions

In the Gospel of Luke, Jesus calls demons serpents and scorpions. When God opens your spiritual eyes, you may see demons at work that have the form of large serpents or small black serpents with big heads. It is important that God reveals to you what they are doing and allows you to see or know what is going to happen to those serpents. I have often seen the angels of God released to take them away as I pray. Realize that the king serpent or dragon is the devil. Revelations 12:9 says, "The great dragon was hurled down—that ancient serpent called the devil, or Satan, who leads the whole world astray. He was hurled to the earth and his angels with him" (NIV).

God is in control of Satan and his demons. The angel who fights Satan or is over Satan is Michael and his angels (Rev. 12:7). Jesus is over all demons. In the gospels, he cast out Legion, which means there were many. Legion controlled the region of the Geresenes (Mark 5:1), but the dwelling of these evil spirits was in the man and in the cemetery. Jesus sets this man free, but left those demons in the region or area (Mark 5:10). They pleaded with him not to send them to the abyss, so they entered and stayed in the water or lake where they drowned the herd of pigs who were two thousand in numbers (Mark 5:13). For some reason, Jesus did not kick them out of the region.

As I was walking around a church, I prayed for the land in order to break any connection with the demonic. I sense that there were some satanic tunnels. The weirdest part was, as I came close to an area of the property, the temperatures suddenly changed in that area. It was cold; I discerned that I was standing on satanic underground tunnel. We begin to pray that God would close and destroy this satanic underground. The confirmation came in a dream I had the next day. I had a dream where I saw a dead black snake next to me. Then as I was outside on the church property, I saw an ugly big head snake going from one side of the ground to the other side. The location was right were we walked and prayed for the property. This demonic snake was causing strife and coming against the leadership of the church. I continued to pray and witnessed a new attitude among the leaders.

Frogs

There are demons that look like frogs in the book of Revelation. Revelation 16:13-14 states, "Then I saw three evil spirits that looked like frogs; they came out of the mouth of the dragon, out of the mouth of the beast and out of the mouth of the false prophet. They are spirits of demons performing miraculous signs, and they go out to the kings of the whole world, to gather them for the battle on the great day of God Almighty"(NIV). In this example, evil begets evil. This is the same principle that we find in Daniel chapter seven, where from the horn other horns grow. Larry Wood, in his article, *Mystery Babylon the Great*, states, "Demons resembling frogs will come out of the mouths of the three. A frog is the symbol of the *kosmokrator* demon (Ephesians 6:12), which empowers politicians in Political Babylon."[2]

These frogs are demons of war. They do signs and miracles so that the kings of the earth will follow their battle strategy and ultimately be led to the last cosmic battle. These demons deceive the kings of the earth to fight God and his angels.

Several years ago, I had a dream of a frog in a small pond in the woods. It was dark in the woods, and I saw this hungry and persistent frog trying to get out of this pond, but somehow I knew it was not its time yet. It moved from one side to the other side of the pond trying to find a way to get out and it could not. I saw around in the woods, and it was dark. Near the pond, I saw this army. It looked like ancient Roman soldiers and they were standing in formation ready for battle. I understood that this frog represented a demon of war and it was ready to be released. Another example of frogs is found in Exodus 8:1-15. Frogs are marine spirits or spirits of the waters. In Exodus 8, Aaron stretches his hands over streams, canals, and ponds, and the plague of frogs begin to invade Egypt. The Egyptian magicians did the same thing—they also made frogs come up on the land of Egypt (Exodus 8:7). The point is that these frogs are spirits of political destruction as described in the book of Revelation and in the example of the plague in Egypt.

Manifestation of Human and Evil Combined

Another demonic animal is the locust. Revelation 9:3 mentions the locusts that are partly human and partly animal. Locusts ascend from the smoke of the bottomless pit to torment humans for six months. The human characteristics are womanlike hair and crowns of gold on their heads. The animal characteristics are teeth like lions' teeth, scales like iron breastplates, and tails like scorpions' tails. Their assignment is to torment people.

One day I felt that something was going on in the spiritual realm and sensed that there was spiritual warfare I needed to do. I felt something heavy in my spirit. I did not like what I was feeling so I called a friend who operates in intercession and who is a seer. This intercessor helped me to sort out in part what I was feeling. In the spiritual realm, she was able to see a "head hunter." My quick reaction was, "a what?" She told me that Satan had released a headhunter to look for me, but it was not finding me. "I see this headhunter and it is in another country in this forest. The soil is rich and that tells me that this demon is in another country. He is systematically looking for you," the intercessor warned me.

As one would imagine, it did not make me feel good to find out that a headhunter was after me. I actually felt paranoid. No wonder those who do not believe in or understand spiritual warfare think that we are paranoid. I thought, "This is crazy!" I was not convinced by this intercessor, so I called another person who can see into the spiritual realm to get confirmation.

I told my friend that something was going on and that I had no peace. My friend was tired and emotionally drained because he had been doing spiritual warfare. He said, "I am going to rest, but I will pray for you." I hung up the phone, and the next day he called me. He told me that after he woke up that morning, he saw a vision.

He saw a vision of a being, half man and half horse—this was weird even for him. I thought, "Great! Things are just getting weirder by the moment." This Greek mythical figure is called centaur. They are caught between the two natures.[3] They are also associated with magic and sorcery.[4] Sometimes, these figures are called archer demons. They are demons of hunting. Once I understood the significance of what his vision confirmed, I prayed that God would cancel the assignment of this being and hide and protect me. Peace returned to me and I knew God had taken care of this head hunter.

When you get these shocking apocalyptic revelations, the enemy and his networks are being unveiled. Satan and his demons obviously do not like this so they look for every chance to take you out. However, the name of the Lord is a strong tower and we can run to him for protection.

The locusts of Revelation and the headhunter are a combination of spiritual and human wickedness. The supernatural is mixed with the natural. Resseguie describes the mixed nature of the locusts, "Animal like characteristics accentuate the ugliness of evil, while humanlike faces accent evil's appearance in human form. Evil's unnaturalness is further illustrated by the abnormal behavior of the locusts."[5] The evil becomes embedded and one with the human nature. God detests and hates this mix of the natural with the supernatural. It goes back to Genesis 6 where the watchers had unnatural sexual relationships with women against God's will. The beings created through the union of the natural and spiritual allow evil to erupt on the earth.

The Antichrist Beast

There are two beasts in Revelations 13--the beast out of the sea and the land beast. New Testament commentators debate about the sea beast—most of them conclude that it is the Antichrist. The role of the land beast is to demand worship of the antichrist. The dragon, Satan will give the beast his power to rule the earth for a period of time. There is a demonic beast that will arise in the end times, but right now the spirit of the antichrist is already at work against Christ, opposing him. The antichrist denies that Christ came in the flesh and is already active in the world (1 John 4:2).

In college, I had a night vision about the nature and the entity of the Antichrist. Due to the intense nature of this vision, I have only shared it with a few close friends. This vision was so shocking that when I woke up I felt that I was still in the vision. As I dreamed, a three-dimensional picture began to unfold in front of my eyes. In the dream, I saw a human body standing. I saw this body from different angles horizontally. Then the vision zeroed in on the top of the body's head. All of a sudden, I saw something like metal slots being removed from the top of the head, and inside of this body I saw an ugly, skinless beast.

Then the night vision shifted to another scene of the beast. This second scene revealed a beast with the head of a cow and no skin to cover the body—I could see the flesh of this beast. Out of the mouth of this beast comes a large endless white tongue. This tongue really surprised and shocked me at the same time. This beast seemed to be confined in an underground tunnel.

The night vision switched to a university campus where I studied my freshman year of college in 1998. I saw two ethnic people who reminded me of Middle Eastern students, walking toward the campus. As I saw them walking to the University, they turned against each other violently and one beat the other brutally, breaking his legs. The nature of these two students was one of rage and vengeance. I woke up thinking of this vivid night vision.

I was intrigued by the vision, so I decided to look up a picture of the Antichrist on the Internet—back in those days, the university only had dial-up internet, so it took a long time for the search engine to bring up any articles and images. When I entered the key word in Spanish, *Anticristo*, it led me to a website in Spain where it showed a skinless cow figure that reminded me of the beast I saw in the dream. I have been trying to locate this website but I have not been successful. However, there are groups in Spain who give their allegiance to the Antichrist.[6] I have often found that research confirms and enlightens revelations that God gives.

I soon began to see the spirit of the Antichrist at work in the world. The September 11 attacks in 2001 caught my attention. *The September 11 Report* outlines in detail how most of the terrorists who flew to the twin towers were student pairs of Arab descendent. This event opened my eyes to see how the spirit of the Antichrist is at work in our world today.

What made this vision more real to me was when the evangelist Perry Stone, Jr., came to a church that I was attending in Ohio. He preached sermons that deviated from the traditional end-time view that the Antichrist will come out from Europe. He boldly preached that the Antichrist would be a fanatical Islamic dictator. Although I did not agree with all of his conclusions, I was reminded of the dream that I had.

In his book, *Unleashing the Beast: How a Fanatical Islamic Dictator Will Form a Ten-Nation Coalition and Terrorize the World for Forty-two Months*, Perry Stone, Jr., states "Today, the crescent moon of Islam is rising. According to their beliefs and traditions, the Islamic religion will one day convert the entire world to Islam. Leading this Islamic revival is the

Mahdi, a coming leader who will assume the role of Messiah. Islamic tradition teaches that Jesus will return and follow the *Mahdi* to Jerusalem, where Jesus will deny that He is the Son of God."[7] This is one point of view regarding the Antichrist. But whatever your view point one thing is for sure, there are signs that the spirit of the Antichrist is using the major religions of the world. Satan does not care about your religion or ethnicity, he just wants to bring death and destruction to humans and oppose God's work.

Apocalyptic Animals

Demonic animals, natural and spiritual beings, and the Antichrist are all a part of Satan's strategies. God also uses animals and other spiritual beings to advance his kingdom and counter Satan's plans. Throughout the book of Revelation there are many characters that worship and act in obedience to God. Jim Resseguie categorizes the animals of heaven as apocalyptic animals. The apocalyptic animals include the four living creatures, the lamb, and eagles. Resseguie states, "Whereas the birds of midheaven are associated with the demonic, the eagle, a magnificent bird of power and speed, is an apocalyptic animal. The eagle flies in midheaven like other birds, but it stands apart from others as a creature of unsurpassed strength and speed."[8] There are three main references in the book of Revelation to the eagle. The first mention of the eagle is found in chapter 4 where the living creatures are described. The second reference is Revelations 8:13, where the eagle announces a quick disaster. The third reference to the eagle is found in Revelation 12:14, where the woman escapes from the dragon on eagles' wings.

Rick Joyner, in his book *The Final Quest*, describes a series of visions that God gave to him. In one of the visions, he relates an account about the eagles of God. The eagles of God are the prophetic eyes to those whom the Lord has given powerful weapons. In the vision one eagle talks to Rick saying, "We have been shown all that Lord is doing, and all that the enemy is planning against you. We have scoured the earth and together we know all that needs to be known for the battle."[9] Rick also recognizes the heart of the eagle—the eagle is able to see through Rick's heart and recognize that he has the same gift as the eagle. God awakened those spiritual gifts in him. The eagle, Rick and those with similar gifts work together with clear communication and do not suffer any loss in the battle against darkness.

Rick asks the eagle where it was coming from. The eagle responds,

"We eat snakes. The enemy is bread for us. Our sustenance comes from doing the Father's will, which is to destroy the works of the devil. Every snake that we eat helps to increase our vision. Every stronghold of the enemy that we tear down strengthens us so we can soar higher and stay in the air longer." The eagle continues, "We have just come from a feast, devouring the serpents of shame who have bound many of your brothers and sisters...They are coming with the eagles we left behind to help them find the way, and to protect them from the enemy's counterattacks."[10] The eagles of God help us in spiritual warfare by providing strength and protection. At times, they also act as messengers and destroy demonic animals.

The activity of apocalyptic animals and animals of Satan in midheaven is established biblically. As my prayer partner and I prayed for the church building I told you about earlier, we came to a room where there were bats hanging on the walls. We prayed that God would kick out these demonic animals. Instantly, in the spiritual realm, we saw an eagle come down and take them away. It may be hard to accept, but this stuff is real. Those who have the apocalyptic anointing will be able to see these animals at work and witness God's victory.

Army of the Lord

There are many references in the Old Testament to the angelic army of the Lord. Greg Boyd, in his book *God at War*, has a section dedicated to demonstrating from the Old Testament that the army of the Lord was on the side of the army of the Israelites and even fought for them. One prime example that Boyd gives is found in 2 Samuel 5:23-24. It says, "You shall go up; go around to their rear, and come upon them opposite the balsam trees. When you hear the sound of marching in the tops of the balsam trees, then be on the alert; for the Lord has gone out before you to strike the army of the Philistines." Boyd boldly declares, "The battle between the Israelites and the philistines was more than a physical battle. 'Marching in the tops of the balsam trees' was 'an army of God' (1 Chron 12:22), his legions of 'mighty ones,' fighting on David's behalf."[11]

The great example of how the army of the Lord protected the prophet Elisha from the army of the Arameans is found in 2 Kings 6:8-23. The Aramean king finds out that Elisha was telling the king of Israel his strategies, so he sent his army to capture him. When Elisha and his servant get up in the morning—his servant panics. Elisha tells him not to worry because there are more with them. 2 Kings 6:17, says, "And Elisha prayed, 'O Lord, open his eyes so he might see.' Then the Lord opened the servant's eyes, and he looked and saw the hills full of horses and chariots of fire all around Elisha" (NIV). Psalms 34:7 says, "The angel of the Lord encamps around those who fear him, and he delivers them." Joshua 5:14 tells us that there is a commander of the army of the Lord. In the case of Elisha, this army causes blindness to the army of the Arameans. This army of the Lord is always watching over his people.

One evening, as I was enjoying God's presence in prayer, I began to feel the presence of the Holy Spirit in an intense way. I just kept worshiping in silence—all of the sudden, in my spirit I saw a whole army of angels walking to assault the strongholds of the enemy in this region. I was in awe of this army. They marched and came to this place and were waiting for orders. What was amazing is as they were waiting for the major assault against the enemy, they were positioned strategically ready for unexpected attacks. They all were dressed white, armed with weapons, and ready for battle. I knew that God was in control and that this was his battle not mine.

Spiritual Weapons

There are times when God will simply use spiritual weapons without dispatching his army. It is intriguing to see spiritual warfare in the book of Genesis. Genesis 3:24 says, "After he drove the man out, he placed on the east side of the Garden of Eden cherubim and a flaming sword flashing back and forth to guard the way to the tree of life." Some people might want to believe this was a one time, but protection from God may manifest the same way today. God not only placed powerful angels to protect the Garden, but he also stationed a flaming sword that went back and forth protecting the entrance into the garden. Angels did not handle the sword; the flaming sword was sent by God to protect the Garden.

God sometimes uses different weapons to defeat the diverse forces of evil. The afternoon, as we were praying in the church, God began to reveal different demonic animals, and the different weapons and tactics of God. In the spirit realm, a big frog was sitting in one corner of the building—we prayed that God would destroy it. In the spiritual realm, we saw two swords fall and pierce each side of this frog and cut it in half. The Lord sent fire to destroy the frog. I never imaged that I would be writing about spooky stuff like this. It is still weird and hard for my mind to accept. Nevertheless, the Lord showed it to me, and I know it is real as weird as it sounds. God does use swords to come against these demonic forces.

Another weapon that God showed me was the offensive use of the shield. Paul makes a reference to "take up the shield of faith" (Ephesians 6:16)(NIV). Although, shields are primarily a defensive weapon of protection, they can be used as an offensive weapon. Think of those movies that depict epic battles. When a seasoned soldier is in hand-to-hand combat, his shield is not just there for him to hide behind. He will use it to bash in heads and take out whatever comes within arms length.

While in prayer for the church building God instructed me to release golden shields to come against his enemies, and I saw them being released into the spiritual realm. The first time he spoke to me to pray for shields, I was unsure but obeyed anyway. After I prayed in faith, the Lord allowed me to see how they came down and destroyed his enemies. There were many little golden sharp shields being released in the spiritual realm; they cut through a thick oppression that filled the room.

Another time, I was under spiritual attack, and was feeling emotionally and spiritually drained. I felt led by the Spirit to pray to God for protection. All the sudden, I began to pray for God to release a shield around my house. I immediately felt peace and sensed the strong power of God. In the spirit, I could see a big golden shield protecting our home.

Scripture, personal experience, and the collaborative experiences of others confirm the reality of demonic and apocalyptic animals. Obviously, these revelations of animals and spiritual weapons are not given to everybody. Whether we see into the spiritual realm or not, it is good to be aware of the supernatural and always listen to God's instructions. Those who have their eyes open to this realm need to seek mature people to help discern their experience.

The reason that we need to be aware of these demonic beings is that our prayers are powerful to destroy their evil work here on earth. They all have specific assignment, and their assignment is all about the destruction of human beings. God waits for us to align our wills with his will so his kingdom will manifest on earth. The Lord's Prayer is that his will be done on earth as it is in heaven. God's work is always to build, redeem, restore and bless his people. As our prayers come into agreement with his will, we will see the forces of darkness defeated and God's work manifest.

Dangers of Spiritual Warfare

There are many dangers when you engage in the supernatural. Once the gifts of the Spirit begin to operate, the emphasis can shift away from what God is doing to what Satan is doing. I have met many Christians who are obsessed with Satan. When the obsession takes control of the person, the demons that they are fighting can easily oppress them. When you engage the enemy, he will take advantage of any situation. It is wise to be coached by a mentor, a pastor or someone who is experienced with this calling.

Another danger is that God reveals things for us to pray about and wants us to wait for his guidance. Often, it is not the revelation or information that we obtain from God that gets us in trouble, but what we do with that information that can take us away from where God is working. For instance, if you are ministering in a place where the gifts of the Spirit are not welcome, then you have to be careful to listen to the Spirit before moving in any revelation that God gives you. Certainly, God gives revelation, but if the people are not open then the best thing is to pray for a breakthrough without revealing what God showed you. The exception would be when the Spirit tells you to reveal to them what He showed you. Even then, attacks will come your way, but if you listen to the Spirit, he will give you a way out! If you disobey and do something that God did not tell you to do, then you need to acknowledge your disobedience and repent. You might still deal with consequences even if you repent.

Assisting Others in Warfare

I remember when I first started to do spiritual warfare. One evening, I was alone, and all of a sudden I heard claws scratching on the side of the roof. I heard it but I could not see the demons that were harassing me. I was new to spiritual warfare and did not know what to do—I was under attack. All of a sudden, I thought to call my pastor and tell him what was going on. First, on the phone he agreed and prayed with me in rebuking those demons away. Second, he taught me to stand strong and learn how to rebuke them. The important thing that I learned from this attack is that we are not alone in this fight. There are others fighting against these forces. We need to receive the help of other intercessors and prayer warriors.

Growing up in church, I have come in contact with many different kinds of intercessors and prayer warriors—some are more trained and equipped than others. Two intercessors who have impacted my life are my mother and a worship leader who are dedicated to keep a consistent life of prayer in the morning. Intercessors, prayer warriors, and those who are intuitively in tune with the Holy Spirit can navigate in the spiritual realm. They are acquainted and familiar with the supernatural work of the Holy Spirit in their lives, and the life of the church.

Since these types of people can be spiritually sensitive to the ongoing work of the Holy Spirit, they are able to see when others are in trouble, or might need prayer or deliverance. Intercessors are the support of the pastor, the local church, and the kingdom of God. Through revelations of the Spirit and spiritual burdens they pray on behalf of those that God is working with, and protect them against the forces of evil.

Wherever the light of Christ is shinning, darkness is present and Satan keeps account of the work of God among his people. When God gives spiritual gifts to his children, the enemy will come and try to steal them. By confusing their minds he will try to keep them from spiritual growth. The enemy does not want us to be spiritually trained to distinguish the work of the Spirit, or understand apocalyptic symbolism. The moment we recognize how God is operating and working in us, the enemy knows that we are going to be dangerous. Therefore, the enemy will attack the experienced warrior and intercessor and will try to keep the new warriors and intercessors from growing in their gifts.

I remember when God began to teach me about the anointing of the Spirit and the gifts, the enemy tried to distract me from growing. One night, God gave me a dream in which I saw a black pit bull dog eating precious blue pearls that I had in my hands. I understood that the enemy was trying to take away and come against the spiritual gifts that God was giving me. The most important thing was that I had a pastor who was always praying for my spiritual growth. He never told me that he was praying for me, but I am sure that his prayers were protecting me.

Notes

1. Eckhardt, John. *Prayers That Rout Demons.* Lake Mary: Charisma House, 2008. Page, 65.
2. Wood, Larry. *Mystery Babylon the Great: The Armageddon War.* http://www.biblenews1.com/babylon/babylon8.html Date: May 12, 2008
3. http://en.wikipedia.org/wiki/Centaur
4. http://www.enchantedkingdom.co.uk/Bestiary/Centaurs.htm

5. Resseguie, 119.
6. Kaosenlared.net. http://www.kaosenlared.net/noticia.php?id_noticia=32324 Date: September 27, 2007.
7. Stone, Perry. *Unleashing the Beast: How a Fanatical Islamic Dictator Will Form a Ten-Nation Coalition and Terrorize the World for Forty-Two Months*. (Cleveland: Pathway Press, 2003), 13.
8. Ibid, 135.
9. Joyner, Rick. *The Final Quest* (New Kingston: Whitaker House, 1996), 58.
10. Ibid, 59-60.
11. *God at War*, 133.

6

Third-Level Spiritual Warfare

I was seeking God's face one evening and sensed him saying, "I am going to teach you third level spiritual warfare." I had never heard that term before. I began to think, *what does this all mean?* I did not know what first or second level spiritual warfare were, let alone third. I was in for a surprise! I asked myself these questions: How was the Lord going to train me in this fight? Am I ready to be the warrior that God is calling me to be?

I would like to tell you that, after he spoke this, I began to fast and practice spiritual disciplines, but I did not. Rather I went about my life and ministry, but God kept his word. That month he interrupted my life and began to pour out revelatory knowledge in dreams and visions. I was having constant dreams and visions through which God was showing me strategically where the enemies that were hindering his work were posted.

In a dream, God showed me the region in which I was ministering. As mentioned earlier, I saw a black horse, a strong man sitting on the horse, and above the strong man a principality. These were connected and moved together. They were in an area that seemed to be gray and black. I came to their camp in this night vision, and they knew that I was in their camp, but they could not see me. All of a sudden, a light hit the other side of the camp, and they left me alone, thinking that I was not there. I learned that whenever light hits, the enemy watches to see what God is doing.

I heard the principality and the strong man talking, but I could not distinguish what they were saying. I was in the middle of their camp, and they did not see me. This was when God opened my eyes and taught me that he is in control of the principalities. I learned that when he calls you to do apocalyptic warfare he gives a covering. As you are obedient, the enemy cannot touch you unless God allows it to happen. The covering is amazing, and one is able to cover others because of the authority and covering that God has given you. This was my introduction to third level spiritual warfare.

Levels of Warfare

Third-level spiritual warfare engages the enemy on a regional stage. This level of warfare utilizes specific weapons and strategies to combat Satan's regional tactics. It uncovers the principalities and the demons that control a certain region. This is accomplished by relying on the power and leading of the Holy Spirit. This is different from coming against demons that are oppressing or possessing individuals. It is not about personal deliverance, but about setting geographical regions free. Through the revelatory gifts of word of the knowledge, word of wisdom, discernment, and prophecy, which often manifest through visions, dreams, and the still small voice of the Holy Spirit, we are able to see the devil's schemes. The apocalyptic anointing fosters these spiritual gifts within the believer's life, but, when engaging in warfare, it is necessary to understand proper authority.

Understanding Proper Authority

The first thing to learn about spiritual warfare is authority. We need to understand what kind of authority Christ has given us, and most importantly allow the Lord and his authority to come against the forces of darkness. After all, it is his fight not ours—we just join him in the process. Second, the Lord has the ultimate say in spiritual warfare, especially when you are dealing with principalities. Third, do not take on authority that Christ has not given you, or you will be destroyed.

Since we are sitting in heavenly places with Christ, we are above demonic forces. Nevertheless, Christ is the one who deals with the principalities and powers, not us. He has the power to destroy them. We get to witness and sometimes participate, but ultimately he confronts them. For example, God gave me a dream where I was transferring from a mini van to a tourist bus. Someone opened the door for me and I walked onto the tourist bus. I went and sat down in the only seat that I could see. The seat looked like a first class airplane seat. I sat down to relax as somebody else drove the bus. Although I did not see the driver, I know God was the driver and not me. In spiritual warfare, Christ is the conductor or the driver; we just enjoy the ride and when he tells us, we obey.

Two primary scriptures teach us that God is the only one who rebukes Satan. The first is found in Zechariah and the other is found in the book of Jude. Zechariah 3:2, states, "The Lord said to Satan, 'The Lord rebukes you, Satan! The Lord, who has chosen Jerusalem, rebukes you! Is not this man a burning stick snatched from the fire?" The Lord is rebuking Satan in the name of the Lord. Only Christ can dethrone these principalities. Consider Jude 1:8-10, which says:

> In the very same way, these dreamers pollute their own bodies, reject authority and slander celestial beings. But even the archangel Michael when he was disputing with the devil about the body of Moses, did not dare to bring a slanderous accusation against him, but said 'the Lord rebuke you!' Yet these men speak abusively against whatever they do not understand; and what things they do understand by instinct, like unreasonable animals—these are the very things that destroy them. (NIV)

I Give You Authority, by Charles H. Kraft, says spiritual authority, "then, is part of who we are. It is recognized by God and by the enemy world as flowing from our very beings."[1] Kraft goes on to say that the authority that God gives us is not just an authority based on our position of leadership. Rather, the Spirit uses the leader's personality, gifting, and character. This evolves out of a deep relationship with God. Pastors, however, can also influence the spiritual realm because of their position. Kraft says, "The position of pastor also involves leaders in activity that carries great impact in the spiritual realm. The authority granted at the human level through ordination is taken seriously by the spirit world, whether or not the pastor has the proper gifting to fill the office."[2] I believe that this principle applies to other positions as well. Those given power and authority in the natural realm also have greater authority in those areas in the spiritual realm. This may include presidents of organizations, CEOs, administrators, teachers, parents over their children, and positions of responsibility. The key is to recognize what kind of authority Jesus has given us to do ministry.

The authority of God is delegated to his people. We not only obey and submit to God directly, but we obey and submit to the leaders that God has placed in our lives. Sometimes delegated authority is in conflict with God's authority. Watchman Nee says, "When delegated authority (men who represent God's authority) and direct authority (God himself) are in conflict, one must render submission but not obedience to the delegated authority."[3] When conflicts arise, one has to be aware not to disobey or even disrespect leadership. If we are not careful, our words and actions may allow the enemy to take advantage of the situation. Rebellion can easily manifest in our hearts during this stage, and when rebellion is at work, the enemy has an easy foothold to come against us. If you find yourself in a situation where the leadership is acting outside of God's will and you can no longer respectfully submit, then you must leave—alone. A good book that deals with these issues is *A Tale of Three Kings* by Gene Edwards.

Terry Nance, in his book, *God's Armor Bearer,* describes the proper conduct of those who understand and value delegated authority. Nance believes that the one who understands proper authority is the one who supports their leader, and supports and submits to one another. Nance states, "Most Christians do not understand the true meaning of submission to authority. 'Oh, but I will always submit myself to God!' This is a comment I hear quite often...anything less than full submission is rebellion, and rebellion is the principle on which Satan and his kingdom operate."[4]

Consider the example of comprehending proper authority in the life of the centurion. The faith of the centurion is based upon the proper understanding and submitting to the authority of the words of Jesus. Matthew 8:8-9, says, "The centurion replied, "Lord, I do not deserve to have you come under my roof. But just say the word, and my servant will be healed. For I, myself, am a man under authority, with soldiers under me. I tell this one, 'Go,' and he goes; and that one, 'Come,' and he comes. I say to my servant, 'Do this,' and he does it." Jesus approved the faith of this centurion and used him as a model for obeying the commands of Jesus. The centurion understood that authority gives us a choice of obedience or rebellion.

Rebellion hinders many people from doing effective ministry in the local church. The apocalyptic anointing has the power to demolish the stronghold of rebellion because it sees God's direct or delegated authority through the eyes of discernment. Nance's book is helpful for those who want to do ministry in the local church—he gives them careful biblical guidance in how to develop their ministry within the local church. Rebellion gives a foothold to the devil to dwell in certain places.

The Cleansing of the Temple

There are times when we need to cleanse the earth and the places of worship from demonic spirits. There are two main examples of temple cleansing in the scriptures: Ezekiel 8 and Mark 11:12-19. In Ezekiel 8

God takes the prophet to see the demonic and pagan worship that the leaders of Israel were practicing. God reveals the sins in the temple and then shows the prophet why his glory is leaving the first temple. Jesus, in the gospel of Mark, cleanses the temple and kicks out all vendors. The temple is for prayer, but they have defiled the temple with their merchandise. Whatever happens in the spiritual manifests in the natural. Ezekiel sees the spiritual darkness of the pagan worship in the holy temple of God, and Jesus sees their deceitful and greedy hearts. Both must be cleansed in the spirit and in the natural.

Dr. Henry Malone's book *Portal to Cleansing* says, "Portals—it is a popular word these days…is a door or gate, an approach or entrance to a bridge or tunnel…there are spiritual doorways waiting to be unlocked."[5] According to Dr. Malone, these portals can be opened because of sin committed in the land. He gives a specific scenario where this family was tormented by demons—he is able to discern that the land was dedicated to Satan. He anoints stakes and prays over them so those evil spirits will not come back.

Dr. Malone also mentions that God has portals through which the angels of God travel back forth from the third heaven to earth without any demonic interference. Dr. Malone states, "Portals from God begin in the third Heaven, travel through the second Heaven, and open unto the earth. Portals exist all around the earth (Psalm 24:7; Revelation 4:1-2; Revelation 3:20; Matthew 7:13-14)."[6] These portals could be the branches, or horns that the prophet Daniel and Mary Baxter saw.

When God spoke to me about third-level spiritual warfare, I never imagined what he would have me do. With another person who is insightful in the spiritual realm, I began to receive revelations about a specific area that God wanted to cleanse. Together, we were able to pray and discern. We began to receive revelations about events from the past—remember eternity is outside of our time limitations; in the spiritual realm, what happened centuries ago may be revealed like it happened yesterday. When evil is allowed to enter into a specific place or location, cleansing may need to take place. Words, actions, sins, vows, and other human actions can defile a location or groups of people and give demonic forces a place of influence. Repentance, forgiveness, breaking of vows or curses, and prayer can reclaim groups and places for the will of God.

One revelation that God gave us led me to pray for a piece of land. God showed me there were some men in the early 1800's that cursed the ground. They had made an oath and buried two stakes in the ground. Since I was in spiritual training, I wanted to find the actual stakes. We spent the better part of an hour praying and searching for those two stakes. I kept asking God where they were. We discerned a place, but there were no stakes there. After a length of time the Holy Spirit spoke to me, "Do you really think wooden stakes would have survived the passage of time as the land was developed and used for different purposes?" I felt a little foolish. However, I have found that the revelations that God gives regarding these things are so vivid that I often want to see the reality of what is revealed in the spirit. It is not easy to walk between these two worlds. Although we could not find those stakes, the reality of the damage to the spiritual realm was evident. By faith, we went to the specific location God had shown us earlier, prayed and broke the curses and oaths that were still affecting the region.

This was just the beginning. After we broke the hold of the oath, God began to give me dreams and revelations about demonic snakes. In the Bible, Jesus gave his disciples power against snakes and scorpions and upon all the power of the enemy, and he promised that nothing would harm them (Luke 10). While I received revelations concerning snakes, God actually showed me demons or evil spirits in their original form as dark evil fallen angels. Some of the snakes I saw were territorial spirits.

Territorial Spirits

In *the Handbook of Spiritual Warfare*, Dr. Ed Murphy talks about the tradition of watcher angels: "The name 'angelic watcher' is found in Daniel 4:13, 17, 23 in scripture. Daniel 4 described an 'angelic watcher, a holy one...thus they partly control the affairs of men, and it is also possible they are the territorial spirits..."[7] Historical Jewish literature offers insights to help us further understand territorial spirits. The book of Enoch expounds upon Genesis 6:4, which mentions the origin of the nephilim. Enoch chapters 7-15 talk about the "sons of God" called watchers. The watchers are the fallen angels of God who had sexual relationships with women and whose children became the giants or nephilimswho ate everything including human blood (Enoch 7). The book of Enoch says:

> You being spiritual, holy, and possessing a life which is eternal, have polluted yourselves with women; have begotten in carnal blood; have lusted in the blood of men; and have done as those who are flesh and blood do. These however die and perish. Therefore have I given to them wives, that they might cohabit with them; that sons might be born of

them; and that this might be transacted upon earth. But you from the beginning were made spiritual, possessing a life which is eternal, and not subject to death for ever. Therefore I made not wives for you, because, being spiritual, your dwelling is in heaven. Now the giants, who have been born of spirit and of flesh, shall be called upon earth evil spirits, and on earth shall be their habitation. Evil spirits shall proceed from their flesh, because they were created from above; from the holy Watchers was their beginning and primary foundation. Evil spirits shall they be upon earth, and the spirits of the wicked shall they be called. The habitation of the spirits of heaven shall be in heaven; but upon earth shall be the habitation of terrestrial spirits, who are born on earth. (24) [Note the many implications of vss. 3-8 regarding the progeny of evil spirits]. The spirits of the giants shall be like clouds, (25) which shall oppress, corrupt, fall, content, and bruise upon earth. (25) [The Greek word for "clouds" here, *nephelas*, may disguise a more ancient reading, Napheleim (*Nephilim*)].They shall cause lamentation. No food shall they eat; and they shall be thirsty; they shall be concealed, and shall not (26) rise up against the sons of men, and against women; for they come forth during the days of slaughter and destruction. (26) Shall not. [Nearly all manuscripts contain this negative, but Charles, Knibb, and others believe the "not" should be deleted so the phrase reads "shall rise up"].[8]

Could it be that these giants, who are like the clouds and the circles that Mary Baxter and I saw in the spiritual realm, are the same? Are these the spirits that brought evil upon the earth?

Strongmen

Principalities govern churches through demonic strongman, and people give their allegiance to the dark forces either intentionally or unintentionally, knowingly or unknowingly. Satan gets a hold in a church through his strongman. There are three main scripture references about the strongman: Matthew 12:29, Mark 3:27, and Luke 11:21-22. The gospel of Luke identifies the close relationship between the strong man and an evil spirit. Luke 11:21, 22, 24-26, states, "When a strong man, fully armed, guards his own house, his possessions are safe. But when someone stronger attacks and overpowers him, he takes away the armor in which the man trusted and divides up the spoils... When an evil spirit comes out of a man, goes through arid places seeking rest and does not find it. Then it says, 'I will return to the house I left.' When it arrives, it finds the house swept clean and put in order. Then it goes and takes seven other spirits more wicked than itself, and they go in and live there. And the final condition of that man is worse than the first." Notice that there is an interaction between the forces of darkness and humans. Humans, individuals, and groups can be a dwelling place for evil spirits.

Harold Caballeros, in his book *Victorious Warfare,* questions the identity of the strong man. He says, "My interest was drawn to the word man. Why was that word used so often in the Bible? Why strong man? Why not strong spirit or strong principality or strong power? Why did it have to be specifically man? I began to realize that God was speaking here of the interaction between human beings and the spiritual realm."[9] Harold also believes that there are people who intentionally give themselves to be controlled by principalities through sin, un-forgiveness, jealously, and even the occult. He also believes that there are kings here on earth that rule through demonic forces; however, their focus is on regional control instead of individuals in the congregation.

The demonic realm can influence religious leaders. There are two main examples in the New Testament of this influence on religious leaders. The first one is Matthew 3:7, where John calls the religious leaders "brood of vipers." Later, Jesus also calls them a "brood of vipers" (Matthew 12:34). Brood is a group of young animals, and a viper is a venomous snake who had a single pair of long, hollow fangs and a thick heavy body. Jesus was saying to the religious leaders that they were sons of deadly snakes. In Luke 10:19, Jesus gives authority to his disciples to trample on snakes and scorpions and to overcome all the power of the enemy. Snakes are equated with demons. In reality, Jesus was saying that the religious leaders had become sons of devils.

Jesus, in the book of John, called the religious leaders children of the Devil. John 8:44 says, "You belong to your father, the devil, and you want to carry out your father's desire. He was a murder from the beginning, not holding the truth, for there is no truth in him. When he lies, he speaks his native language, for he is a liar and the father of lies." The devil's character is murder and lying. The religious leaders were lying about Jesus' identity, and they wanted to kill him because they did not believe that he was speaking the truth. The works of a liar are deception and manipulation.

Deception misleads people in appearances and with words. Manipulation manages and influences others in an unfair manner. Deception and manipulation eventually lead to scheming; the development of a systematic plan of action. At times, this could lead to physical murder, but the result could also be emotional or spiritual murder. In the case of Jesus, the schemes of the religious and the demonic forces' took Jesus to the cross. In the local church, religious leaders who are knowingly or unknowingly being control by demonic forces can oust the pastor, divide a congregation, and come against the ministry and mission of the local church. Leaders may even plot against each other. If you do not see love, but hate, jealousy and pride, remember these are works of the flesh (Gal. 5). Their actions can usually be identified as deceptive and manipulative—indicative of the work of a strongman.

Principalities

Paul connects these sorts of schemes with principalities. Ephesians 6:11, says, "Put on the full armor of God so that you can take your stand against the devil's schemes." After teaching the Ephesians to put on the whole armor, Paul then reveals the demonic hierarchy and how Satan uses his demons to scheme against God's people. 2 Corinthians 2:11 says, "in order that Satan might not outwit us. For we are not unaware of his schemes." However, many Christians are not aware of the devil's schemes and naively come into agreement with principalities to destroy the work of God.

In the process of discerning principalities in churches, we must understand how the snakes or strongmen are working. The demonic action mixes with the human flesh. Problems and schemes in congregations may arise out of the flesh and then become demonic, or they could be demonically initiated and then manifest through fleshy Christians. This is the work of the brood of vipers. For example, Rick Joyner talks about how some Christians carry demons and throw arrows at each other when confronted with the truth. Joyner states, "Many of these believers were host to more than one demon, but one would obviously be in charge. It was clear that the power of the demons was rooted almost entirely in the power of deception, but they had deceived these Christians to the point where they could use them and they would think they were being used by God."[10] Demons can and will influence Christians if they do not discern the voice of God.

Pay attention and discern what kind of spirit is operating when there is conflict in the congregation. In all of these matters, it is essential that you continually check your own heart that you do not end up operating in the same spirit you are coming against. Resolving conflict in a congregation is never easy. Many variables play a part in the midst of conflict. There are things in the natural that must be done to resolve conflict such as following Matthew 18, and when appropriate, bringing in a neutral party to restore relationships and ministry. A pastor or leader may need to confront the situation and call it as it is. Jesus modeled this when he named the religious leaders' source, the devil, and he outlined their schemes. It is not easy, but it has to be done. The religious leaders and the demonic powers both needed to be confronted. This must be done in love. Often the preaching of the Word can break down the power behind these schemes.

In most conflicts, I see people trying to appease one another. When demonic forces and the flesh are active, it is never possible to appease either one. The solution is not appeasing people. It is deliverance. If there are demonic powers behind the religious leaders, those religious leaders need deliverance--they need to be set free. It is sad to say, but many people compromise when they should not. They just want to appease the person who is harming the work of the Lord in the church. We must remember that the work of spiritual warfare, and ministry in general, is never about receiving glory and approval from one another, but it is about obtaining approval from the Heavenly Father.

Jesus says to the religious leaders, "How can you believe if you accept praise from one another, yet make no effort to obtain the praise that comes from the only God?" (John 5:45, NIV). The problem is that religious leaders just care about what others think and say about them, and they leave God somewhere else. Their priorities are not right. We need to hear what God says about a particular situation or a particular individual and then minister accordingly. It is not about protecting our own political agenda for the church or protecting somebody else's agenda. Rather, we must be sure that we are listening to heaven. Heaven speaks, and when it speaks, we need to follow the leading of the Spirit of God. God has first place. The people, and even the church, are secondary to the will of God. We hear God, then we do ministry.

Third level spiritual warfare uncovers the work of principalities, and the works of the strong man in individuals, groups, and regions. With proper authority and cleansing people and places from the territorial spirits, the church can move forward to destroy the powers of the devil that try to influence the work of God.

Embracing Third-Level Spiritual Warfare

Everybody is called to do some sort of ministry in the kingdom of God. Paul states, "There are different kinds of gifts, but the same Spirit. There are different kinds of service, but the same Lord. There are different kinds of working, but the same God works all of them in all men. Now to each one the manifestation of the Spirit is given for the common good" (1 Corinthians 12:4-7). The Spirit gives gifts and callings to God's people. The apocalyptic anointing is recognized in our lives when the Spirit makes us sensitive to the spiritual realm. God makes us sensitive to the presence and power of the Holy Spirit. The gospel of John describes the in-working power of the Holy Spirit as "streams of living waters flowing within" the believer (John 7:38). Next, the Spirit of God begins to give us the ability to distinguish what demonic activity is taken place around us. It is interesting that spiritual gift inventories ask specific questions about whether you see dreams, visions, and demons.

The people who are called to the apocalyptic anointing often are those who are naturally aware of the spiritual realm. For example, some children are more aware of spiritual things than others. Recent charismatic writers are beginning to tell stories of when they were kids and were able to perceive the spiritual world and speak prophetically of the future. They frequently freaked out their parents because of the things that they know.

I believe these children have an authentic gift of God. If the church is not able to embrace their gifts and provide training, some will suppress the gift or find other places where it is received. Without biblical foundation, these individuals may become fascinated with the dark side. They will be enticed by the enemy and use their gift for personal gain and for the work of lying spirits.

Unfortunately, for many Christians who have the ability to see in the spiritual realm, if those gifts are not correctly nurtured, the enemy and the mental health professionals can hinder God's work and send these Christians to institutions. I have met people who have this apocalyptic anointing and do not have a background in their churches that teaches about the supernatural work of the Holy Spirit—often, they are misunderstood and even clinically misdiagnosed.

The greatest danger I see is that these spiritually gifted people are drawn to the supernatural like the occult or New Age movement. The reason is that Christianity has not been open to the subjective work of the Spirit. In other words, there is no room for them in many institutional churches. Things are changing—more churches are beginning to understand the role of Holy Spirit and spiritual gifts. The church must provide a safe and appropriate place to explore the supernatural, teaching about the Holy Spirit and allowing his gifts to manifest.

Dealing with Principalities

In the spiritual warfare conference 2006[11] hosted by Morningstar Ministries, Rick Joyner spoke about how to deal with principalities. Whenever he goes to a different region or country people ask him to identify and tell them about the ruling principalities that are over their cities, regions, or country. He hesitates to tell them. Every time he has exposed principalities, something bad happens that is connected with them. If he does reveal the principality in their city, it is because certain principalities have a hold on the believers of that region, and God wants to set them free. We have power to cast demons out of people, in first level of spiritual warfare, but principalities are another level and a different realm. We must be cautious.

It is important to obey God if he is revealing principalities to you. You must listen and do what he tells you when dealing with principalities. If he tells you to go somewhere else for a day, do it. The battle may start, and you could be caught between the angels of God and the principalities. For example, one day when I was engaged in spiritual warfare for a region, God woke me up around 3:00 a.m. He told me to leave the city until he let me know I could return. I did not like that, but we obeyed and we left. While in prayer, my wife saw a serpent coming around the house looking for us. God took care of that serpent.

Often God gives us revelations to warn us of danger. In Matthew 2:12, the Magi are warned in a dream not to return the same way, because Herod wanted to kill baby Jesus. In Mathew 2:13, an angel speaks in a dream to Joseph to leave Israel and flee to Egypt. After Herod dies, the angel appears to Joseph telling him to return to Israel. God sometimes requires us to move physically or geographically for a certain time, because he knows that we might be in danger. He knows best!

It did not make any logical sense to leave our house, but God was ready to deal with the principality, and he did not want us to be collateral damage. The same night, God warned me of possible attacks from people in the church that the enemy was using to destroy our ministry. Glad to say, God prevented and minimized these attacks because I was obedient to his voice.

Notes

1. Kraft, H. Charles. *I Give You Authority* (Grand Rapids: Baker Books House, 2001), 45.
2. Ibid, 261.
3. Nee, Watchman. *Spiritual Authority* (New York: Christian Fellowship Publisher, 1972), 108.
4. Nance, Terry. *God's Armor Bearer: Serving God's Leaders*. Volume 1 and 2 (Springdale: Focus on the Harvest, 1990), 19.
5. Malone, Henry. *Portals to Cleansing* (Irving: Vision Life Publications, 2005), 37.
6. Ibid, 42-43.
7. Murphy, Ed. *The Handbook for Spiritual Warfare* (Nashville: Thomas Nelson, 2003), 223.
8. http://www.johnpratt.com/items/docs/enoch.html Text and commentary. Emphasis mine.
9. Caballeros, Harold. *Victorious Warfare* (Nashville: Thomas Nelson, 2001), 143.
10. Joyner, Rick. *The Final Quest* (New Kingston: Whitaker House, 1996), 18-19.
11. http://store.morningstarministries.org/cgi-bin/morning/CC67-100. Discerning Principalities and Powers (MP3 Format Sermon)—Rick Joyner and Bob Jones. Deliverance and Spiritual warfare Conference 2006.

7

Walking in the Apocalyptic Anointing

The process of spiritual formation is necessary to function in the apocalyptic anointing. The misconception is that, since God has given us gifts, we do not need to worry about cultivating our gifts spiritually or intellectually. As I prepared to go to college, some of my friends and brothers in Christ put the fear of God in me. They told me that I was going to lose my spiritual life by going to college or seminary. The slogan often recited was "You are going to seminary--we mean cemetery." I did not give in to that fear, and I found out that they themselves were missing something. That something was the chance to develop the gift of the intellect along with the spiritual gifts.

One can grow several ways spiritually. One's priority regarding spiritual growth depends on church background. Many books out there focus on different aspects of the believer's growth. The apocalyptic anointing requires a holistic kind of growth and maturity in God.

Many spiritual disciplines such as prayer, fasting, and Bible study can lead to growth. The question is how one develops his/her spirit, soul, and body. In other words, how do we nurture our spirit so we can enter into the spiritual realm where God is? We will consider the necessity of spiritual formation. Pentecostals often focus exclusively on Holy Spirit baptism and are uninformed or skeptical of spiritual formation.

Spiritual Formation Process

Many seminaries offer spiritual formation and spiritual direction classes. They teach about the Christian's spiritual life—how both clergy and laity need to understand and develop their spirits. I was blessed to be able to take some of these seminary classes.

M. Robert Mulholland, Jr., in his book *Invitation to a Journey*, describes spiritual formation that is, "*1) a process 2) of being conformed 3) to the image of Christ 4) for others.*"[1] In a fast-paced world, there is within Christianity the expectation for God to do something quick—a swift work from brokenness to being perfect in a matter of seconds. I do believe that God can do that, but more often our spiritual life is *a process*.

Mulholland declares, "Often our spiritual quest becomes a search for the right technique, the proper method, the perfect program that can immediately deliver the desired results of spiritual maturity and wholeness."[2] The process of spiritual maturity is linked to the physical growth of an individual—they are stages from infant to toddler, from a toddler to preschooler and so on and so forth. Everyday, every person is in the process of formation—they conduct their lives according to their awareness of the word of God in their decisions and behavior.

The second definition of spiritual formation is *being conformed*. Mulholland continues saying, "spiritual formation is a process of being conformed to the image of Christ, a journey into becoming persons of compassion, persons who forgive, persons who care deeply for others and the world, persons who offer themselves to God to become agents of divine grace in the lives of others and their world—in brief, persons who love and serve as Jesus did."[3] There are two main obstacles one needs to overcome in this stage: one is manipulation, and the other is control. "Manipulators strongly reject being shaped by God. Controllers are inherently incapable of yielding control to God,"[4] states Mulholland. In spiritual formation, God is in control, not us—there is a reversal that happens. God can use us powerfully when we are free from manipulation and control. When we serve God and fight the forces of darkness, we have to be under God's covering to demolish the strongholds of wickedness.

The third part of spiritual formation is to be conformed *to the image of Christ*. We find our identity in the image of Christ. The work of Christ in this process confronts us with our un-Christlike behavior. Mulholland states, "God is there, in grace, offering us the forgiveness, the cleansing, the liberation, the healing we need to begin the journey toward our wholeness and fulfillment in Christ."[5]

Finally, the last part of the definition of spiritual formation is *for the sake of others*. Mulholland describes: "All God's work to conform us to the image of Christ has its sole purpose that we might become what God created us to be in relationship with God and with others."[6] This is centered on the greatest command to love God and to love one another, which is found in Mark 12:30-31. The vertical and horizontal relationships need to be in their proper place. The vertical relationship is with

God—we need to love God with everything that we have. One of the characteristics of a vertical relationship with God is visible when Christians know who they are in Christ. Christians understand they were created in the *Imago Deo*, in the image and likeness of Christ.

As disheartening as it can be, many Christians do not have a Christ-like identity. They have their ethnic and family identity, but not the Christ's identity. They have the high-tech identity but not the raised Christ's identity. In other words, they have other identities except the identity that will get them close to experiencing Christ in rich and glorious ways. Since they do not have Christ's identity, they fall into the identity of the flesh (Galatians 5). Therefore, they envy, try to control each other, and even destroy their fellow Christians. Christianity no longer becomes a vehicle of freedom and liberation, but one of control and fear.

Paul knew the urgent need the New Testament believers had for Christ to be formed in them, so that they would imitate him as he was imitating Christ. The Greek word *imitation* is to mimic. In 1 Thessalonians 1:6, Paul says, "You became *imitators* of us and the Lord; in spite of great suffering, you welcomed the message with the joy given by the Holy Spirit." The person who is rooted in Christ will not quit easily—those who are not will run away quickly.

Colossians 2:6 says, "So then, just as you received Christ Jesus as Lord, continue to live in him, rooted and built up in him, strengthened in the faith as you were taught and overflowing with thankfulness." The key is to continue to be rooted in Christ, and not be rooted by any sorts of traditions. How do we stay rooted in Christ? "Set your minds on things above, not on earthly things. For you died, and your life is now hidden with Christ in God" (Colossians 3:2-3). It is all about keeping our eyes on Jesus who is sitting at the right hand of the Father. As we continue looking up to him, we do not live for ourselves, but we live to please him.

The moment that we take our eyes from where Jesus is sitting, we fall into spiritual idolatry. Spiritual idolatry is making people to be in our image and likeness. We want people to look like us, to smell like us, and to think as we do. When people do not think as we do, we become agents of destruction and condemnation. Coldness and hardness are the fruits of self-induced spiritual idolatry. The love of God is no longer evident—the horizontal relationship becomes fragmented and even destructive.

Some people might say 'I love God,' but, when it comes to loving their fellow brothers and sisters in Christ, they do not show the love that they profess toward Christ. This equation of love does not add up. Love of God plus love of others equals the perfect vertical and horizontal relationships, demonstrating the great commandment found in the gospels. You cannot say you love God and hate your brother—it does not work that way!

1 John 4:18 says, "There is no fear in love. But perfect love drives out fear, because fear has to do with punishment. The one who fears is not made perfect in love." True relationship, whether it is vertical or horizontal, is based upon the perfect love of God. Self-induced spiritual idolatry is based upon punishment, which leads to an awful life of fear and worries. Christians who do not have the Christ-like identity of love have the identity of fear and punishment. These people are the ones who are ready to throw the first stone when someone makes a mistake. Therefore, they need to be transformed by the word of God.

M. Robert Mulholland, Jr., in his book *Shaped by the Word: the Power of Scripture in Spiritual Formation*, makes the distinction between informational reading and formational reading of the scriptures.[7] Informational reading is about covering as much information as quickly as possible to separate the wheat from the chaff and get the data needed to do what must be done. Informational reading is linear—for example, Revelation 17-22 is intended to be seen as three facets of a single vision, and not as a timetable to three different events, but it is one profound vision.

Informational reading seeks to master the text, and, in mastering it, to manipulate the scriptures according to our purposes, intentions, or desires. This kind of reading leads to analytical, critical, and judgmental study of the scriptures, which moves toward a problem solving mentality that feeds back to the functional mode of existence.[8] This prime example of how the soul uses the scriptures in the faculty of the mind is a tendency of many Christians. This kind of reading does not allow God to speak or transform us.

Formational reading is the opposite of informational reading. First, formational reading is not about how much material one can cover in our devotions and reading of scriptures; it is more concerned with quality than quantity. In reading the scriptures, one might read one word, sentence, paragraph, or even a page, but no more than that. Mulholland states, "The point is meeting God in the text."[9] Second, formational reading is not about linear or logical progression of the scriptures, but it is about the depth of the word of God. Mulholland explains, "You seek to allow the passage to open to you its deeper dimension, its multiple layers of meaning."[10] Third, we allow the word or the text to master us, rather than the other way around. We do not tell the word of God what to do. The word of God tells us how to obey our God.

This leads to the fourth point on formational reading: We are the objects that need to be shaped. We do not shape the word of God; the word of God shapes us in the image and likeness of Christ. "Fifth, instead of the analytical, critical, judgmental approach of informational reading, formational reading requires a humble, detached, receptive, loving approach," declares Mulholland.[11] This allows God to penetrate our lives with his holy scriptures—we move from questioning the text to allowing the text to transform our hearts. Finally, formational reading is not about solving problems but about openness to the mystery that we call God. God is the one that solves the problems and dilemmas of our lives. This openness toward God can help the believer to allow the Holy Spirit to take them into a healthy and powerful experience in the supernatural realm.

I have found that formational scripture reading brings confirmation to what God reveals through dreams and visions. When we are both grounded in scripture and free to experience the supernatural, we are transformed in God's image. This transformation occurs in prayer and conversation with God and with others.

Principles of Spiritual Direction

David Benner, in his book *Sacred Companion*, defines what spiritual direction is. Benner defines spiritual direction as "a prayer process in which a person seeking help in cultivating a deeper personal relationship with God meets with another for prayer and conversation that is focused on increasing awareness of God in the midst of life experiences and facilitating surrender to God's will."[12] It is the continued awareness of God in one's life that allows our spiritual growth to flourish in mature ways. One cannot be a lone ranger; we need to have someone who will help keep us accountable. There is great insight, revelation and power with the apocalyptic anointing. Therefore, it is very important to have someone in whom to confide. We not only need to confide in some else, but we also need to trust and practice the presence of God in our lives.

There are two common ways that we can practice the presence of God. The first one is meditation, and the other is contemplation. Meditation is a cognitive process; it is an exercise of the mind that seeks to increase knowledge through serious reflection. Meditation utilizes the study of Scripture and other devotional material in an orderly and prayerful manner.[13]

Contemplation is more affective than cognitive because it is more of an exercise of the heart than of the mind. Contemplation seeks increased openness, awareness, and love for God. The soul is at rest with God, does not require texts to study, and it does not seek to think in an orderly fashion.

There are four disciplines in the curriculum of Christ-likeness: Two disciplines of abstinence and two disciplines of positive engagement. The first one is solitude—a lengthy time of being out of contact with people; second is silence—to escape from sounds and noises, other than the gentle ones of nature. In the discipline of positive engagement, the first one is study—concentrated attention of God and words of scripture; second is worship—praise and reverence for God. These disciplines imprint on our complete being the reality of that which we study.

Those who have the gifts and want to walk in the apocalyptic anointing, need to incorporate spiritual formation into their Christian life. The apocalyptic anointing will have greater impact if we are conform to the image of Christ for the sake of others. If we are renewed by the reading, and studying of the word, where the word will transform us, then we will become agents of transformation. This anointing will flow without any personal hindrance to bless others if we continue to follow the path of spiritual formation.

Few Workers in the Ministry

Although I believe that the Holy Spirit calls every Christian to some sort of ministry, the reality is that the workers are few. We must acknowledge the need for people who are gifted and called. During his ministry, Jesus recognized the need for workers. Matthew 9:35-38 states, "Jesus went through all the towns and villages, teaching in their synagogues, preaching the good news of the kingdom and healing every disease and sickness. When he saw the crowds, he had compassion on them, because they were *harassed* and *helpless*, like sheep without a shepherd. Then he said to his disciples, "The harvest is plentiful but the workers are few. Ask the Lord of the harvest, therefore, to send out workers into his harvest field" (NIV, emphasis mine).

In this passage, Jesus acknowledged that many things harass people. One of them was sickness, and Jesus met that need by healing many. Today, many problems continue to harass people. Bill Hybel says, "I do not need to waste words, making a case for the evil in our world. For the brokenness. For the pain. For the wars. For poverty. For hunger. For hatred. For greed. For broken families. For the neglected elderly. For loneliness. For abuse of the environment."[14] There are many external forces pressing against people, causing them to be in a state of weariness and panic.

Jesus also recognized that people are helpless. People are physically, emotionally, and spiritually harassed by internal or external struggles. They cannot free themselves, so God sends his workers to bring freedom. With the apocalyptic anointing, we are empowered and gifted by the Holy Spirit to bring freedom and deliverance to the harassed.

Once these workers are released to do ministry in the local church, be assured that revival is around the corner. Once people are free from bondages, they will begin to hear God for themselves. God will begin to speak to them about repentance. God will work within them to reconcile sins of the past and present. There will be a conviction in their hearts about the working of the Holy Spirit in their lives.

Embracing the Past, Present, and The Future in Ministry

Looking back, one of the hardest things for me to do was to engage in ministry. When one begins to do ministry, the daunting task is to embrace God's gifting, embrace your identity, and embrace the people that God chooses for you to serve and love. I used to hear college students enthusiastically shout and pray, "Lord, I am going to go change the world for you." Then they went into churches, and a strong resistance rose up against them. What happened to that enthusiasm that they demonstrated in college when the patriarchs of the church challenged them? All of a sudden, their prayer changed from, "Lord, help me change the world" to "Lord, get me out of here!"

Ministry is not what you want it to be, but it is defined by the gifts the Lord has given you. I did not go to college and seminary just to go back and work in a church to appease people and maintain the status quo. The early visions and dreams about spiritual warfare were not something I asked for or sought after. I intentionally avoided talking with people about them. In fact, I ran away from spiritual warfare for several years. I wanted God to use me, but not in that way. It was creepy and scary stuff and came with a high price. Finally, I quit running, embraced it, and let me tell you—God has blessed me tremendously.

Embracing your background and your identity is not easy. I come from a poor family. Broken and misplaced, I lived in three different countries. That is something that I do not like to talk about; however, it is a part of my past. I am finding it easier to minister to those with experiences similar to mine. When God comes and heals your past, you can bring the same healing to others who need it.

Embracing your future is also difficult because it is in God's hands. The future is beyond our control, and we cannot know what God might bring to our life, family, career, or ministry. God will steer you the way he wants you to go, not the way you want to go. He will show you his direction in how to do ministry, how to conduct your life, and how he wants you to develop your gifting.

If you had told me a few years ago that I was going to be ordained with the American Baptist Churches USA, I would have called you "el loco," the crazy one. The most difficult choice in starting my ministry was whether or not to get ordained. My question to the Lord was, "But where, God? I knew that I could not fit within the background that I came from. So now I was faced with a new choice, where do I go to do ministry?

It was a painful experience to leave a denomination that played such a significant role in my early spiritual formation. However, I knew that I could not function with my gifting in that context. The leaders of the American Baptist Churches embraced me, and I chose to leave my former denomination, knowing that I would retain the things that shaped me. Here is the essence of all this, one has to be obedient to move where God can use you as he wants to use you. It is never about a particular denomination or church, it is always about the love of God. He wants to use your gifts and your talents for his glory in whatever context you are placed.

The apocalyptic anointing stems out of the person and work of the Holy Spirit. This anointing is embodied in the life of the believer who wants and is conscious of the Spirit's power and revelatory gifts. The one who carries the apocalyptic anointing must be willing to pursue the call of God in his/her life, willing to pursue spiritual gifts, and willing to be trained in ministry and receive a ministry certificate or degree.

Remembering the Call

We need to understand how to cultivate spiritual gifts, talents, and the experiences God gives us. There are three references in the New

Testament book of 1 Timothy that help us to discern, respond to, and grow in our calling.

The first passage is 1 Timothy 1:18, which says, "Timothy, my son, I give you this instruction in keeping with the prophecies once made about you, so that by following them you may fight the good fight." Here is a good example of how Timothy was inspired to go into ministry. Some prophecies he received encouraged him to follow the path of ministry. Those who gave the prophecies helped him discern his call, and Paul was reminding him of that.

The call of God in your life begins to grow when someone or even God himself gives you an indication that you are called to do a certain ministry. It can be a prophetic word like Timothy received, or a mature Christian may see the call of God. The nurturing of these gifts comes through encouragement, discussion, and friendship.

I recall one Sunday morning during a new member's class when Pastor Gabriel Willis was teaching basic doctrines of the Bible. He looked at me, and smiled. Then he said to me, "the Lord is going to use you in ministry." That was it, and he continued to teach the class. Keep in mind that I was in my preteens, and I had only been saved for six months. All these things were new to me, but that simple word remains in my heart to this day. That simple word kept me focused through Bible College and seminary.

The second scripture reference is 1 Timothy 4:14, it says, "Do not neglect your gift, which was given you through a prophetic message when the body of elders laid their hands on you." Once again, Paul reminds Timothy of his calling. This time, Paul warns him not to neglect his calling when things get hard, but to be a fighter, a good faithful soldier, when opposition comes. The Lord by his Spirit gives gifts, but in order to function properly they need to be affirmed by the body of believers. There are no lone rangers in this world; you need to be connected to a body of believers. Timothy's ministry was launched by the laying on of the hands of the elders.

The third reference is found in 2 Timothy 2:3. Paul says, "Endure hardship with us like a good soldier of Christ Jesus." Ministry is not easy, but the Lord gives the strength and equips us to do ministry. I find that when things get hard in ministry, people, whether they are laity or clergy, begin to neglect their gifts. When people doing ministry get burned out, have bad experiences, or face some kind of hardship like sickness or death; they sometimes choose not to continue to follow God's call in ministry. Paul kept reminding Timothy of his call and to never neglect it or allow circumstances to divert him. I find courage in these verses in my ministry when things are not working out as I expected. Finally, to grow spiritually and intellectually one has to go through the school of the Spirit and through higher education.

The School of the Holy Spirit

Some Christians come from churches where they are able to develop their gifts. They are in an environment where they are able to devoutly seek God's face to be used in ministry. They develop their call to ministry and their gifts by simply allowing God to teach them what they need to do.

Many do not pursue a ministry-focused bachelor's degree let alone a seminary degree. What they find is churches and ministries that offer a two to three year certificate in ministry. Those involved in higher education are alarmed by this and seek to understand it. There are articles trying to explain why ministries and churches are giving them their own training instead of sending them to colleges or seminaries. An argument can be made for both forms of training. However, in order to change people, institutions, and regions, those with the apocalyptic anointing are able to operate in both worlds: the world of the intellect and the supernatural world.

Apocalyptic Anointing: The Case For and Against Higher Education

The apocalyptic anointing with all its spiritual insight and power needs to be accompanied by a developing intellectual life. John Mark Ruthven, in his article, *Are Pentecostal Seminaries a Good Idea*, argues that seminaries are incompetent in training ministers for ministry. Those who go to colleges and seminaries come out confused, uncertain, spiritually cold, and ill equipped. Ruthven, states, "Graduates who became pastors found that 70-80 percent of their seminary education did not apply to their duties in church ministry. Only 48 percent of the students believed that seminary education had impacted their personal life and values to a significant degree."[15] Ruthven, elsewhere, articulates that seminaries, even Pentecostal ones, do not allow for the leading of the Holy Spirit or the prophetic voice of God. He adamantly says, "The central training of Jesus to his disciples, and they to theirs, in faith, prayer, exorcism, and healing, rarely finds a place, in a seminary graduate's transcript, much less as core educational experiences."[16] He gives examples of less academic schools who train leaders to do these works of the kingdom of God.

In response, Joseph L. Castleberry wrote an article, *Pentecostal Seminaries Are Essential to the Future Health of the Church*. He argues that seminaries are good for the sake of theology, psychology, sociology, and spiritual formation. Ministers need to be spiritually-minded but also able to function holistically in the world. Furthermore, he concludes his article by saying, "Best of all, we have founded four Pentecostal seminaries where students can study at high scholarly levels while also being encouraged to be men and women full of the Holy Spirit. Unlike seminarians in all other contexts, students in these schools are free to speak in tongues, lay on hands for healing, offer prophecies, and exercise spiritual gifts—not only in chapel, but occasionally in the classroom as well."[17]

These articles are just a sample of an ongoing debate; Churches and universities believe that their own ministry certificate or degree program is the best. Personally, I believe that both avenues of education are appropriate. The important thing is that education and learning be an ongoing part of the progressive growth of those who carry the apocalyptic anointing. When I began to learn about my gifts, I did not start taking a college class or spiritual formation seminary class. I started developing my gifts and calling in a local church, where my pastor taught biblically about my spiritual gifts. I was strongly encouraged, however, to use the gift of the intellect.

In his book *Full Gospel, Fractured Minds?*, Rick M. Nanez makes a case that Pentecostals/charismatics can accept the gifts of the Spirit such as "the word of wisdom" or "the word of knowledge," where information about real life is revealed in extraordinary ways. He states, however, "Many...seem reluctant to embrace the idea that Christians can glorify God by diligently studying ordinary or religious topics for the sake of mastering them and sharing with others."[18] Daniel and "the boys" are a great example of mixing academics and spirituality: "Not only did God enable these men to learn Babylonian academics 'ten times better' (Dan. 1:20) than the others, but he empowered them to stand spiritually firm in the midst of a radically pagan society."[19] Daniel was a great Old Testament seer, yet he was trained in the academics of the pagan Babylonians. Apocalyptic people today must understand our culture in order to minister effectively in God's kingdom—they need to be educated.

The Spirit plays a major role in giving gifts to Christians. Some gifts are easy to accept, while others are not. The apocalyptic anointing is derived from the Spirit and is pneumatologically-centered. It is important to keep the focus on the giver of the gifts rather than idolizing themselves. The Spirit gives the apocalyptic anointing with the power and revelatory gifts. Intellectually and spiritually the apocalyptic anointing will conquer all the schemes of the devil.

Notes

1. Jr., Robert M. Mulholland, Jr. *Invitation to a Journey* (Downers Grove: InterVarsity Press, 1993), 15).
2. Ibid, 20.
3. Ibid, 25.
4. Ibid, 27.
5. Ibid, 37.
6. Ibid, 40.
7. Mulholland Jr., M. Robert. *Shaped by the Word: The Power of Scripture in Spiritual Formation* (Nashville, Upper Room, 2000).
8. Ibid, 51-53.
9. Ibid, 55.
10. Ibid, 56.
11. Ibid, 59.
12. Benner, David. *Sacred Companion* (Downers Grove: Intervarsity, 2002), 94.
13. Spiritual Direction class notes at Winebrenner Theological Seminary, 2005.
14. Hybel, Bill. *The Volunteer Revolution* (Grand Rapids: Zondervan, 2004), 134.
15. Ruthven, Jon Mark. "Are Pentecostal Seminaries a Good Idea?" *PNEUMA: The Journal of the Society for Pentecostal Studies*—Volume 26, No. 2, Fall 2004: 339.
16. Ibid, 344.
17. Ibid, 353.
18. Nanez, Rick. *Full Gospel, Fractured Minds?* (Grand Rapids: Zondervan, 2005), 30

Selected Bibliography

Amorth, Gabriele. *An Exorcist: More Stories.* San Francisco: Ignatius Press, 2002.

Baxter, Mary. *A Divine Revelation of Hell.* Springdale, Illinois: Whitaker House, 1993.

Boyd, Gregory. *God at War.* Downers Grove, Illinois: Intervarsity Press, 1997.

Macchia, Frank. *Baptized in the Spirit: A Global Pentecostal Theology.* Grand Rapids, Michigan: Zondervan, 2006.

Mounce, H. Robert. *The Book of Revelation.* Grand Rapids, Michigan: Eerdmans Publishing, 1998.

Nee, Watchman. *The Spiritual Man.* New York: Christian Publisher, 1977.

Resseguie, J. L. *Revelation Unsealed: A Narrative Critical Approach to John's Apocalypse.* Leiden: Brill, 1998.

About the Author

Rony M. Reyes holds a bachelor's degree in Pastoral Studies from North Central University, Minneapolis, Minnesota, and a Master's in Theology from Winebrenner Theological Seminary, Findlay, Ohio. Rony is an Ordained Minister with the American Baptist Churches USA, and member of the Society for Pentecostal Studies. Rony Reyes is the Spanish Language Pastor, and Pastor of Missions at North Shore Baptist Church a multicultural church (Anglo, Hispanics, and Japanese) on the North Side of Chicago, Illinois. He writes book reviews on the Pneuma Foundation Journal: Resources for Spirit-empowered Ministry, and has led medical and construction projects in short term mission trips to Central America (Guatemala, El Salvador, and Costa Rica).

Rony was born in Guatemala and as a child moved to the United States. His family settled in Ohio where he met his wife, Hope. The Reyes have two children Gabriel and Olivia.

www.ingramcontent.com/pod-product-compliance
Lightning Source LLC
Chambersburg PA
CBHW031254230426
43670CB00005B/191